W9-CEJ-995

PRAISE

From People Who Really Use
The Sandler Rules

Great combo! David H. Sandler a timeless teacher and Mattson, a current day sales pro ... Don't just read this book, use this book to better your life and the sales profession we all love.

– Anthony Parinello • Author
Selling to VITO • Wall Street Journal Best-seller, *Think and Sell Like a CEO*

If I could choose only one aspect of sales that I learned from Sandler Training that has truly changed my life and sales life it's this ... sales people have rights! I truly never believed that before and let people walk all over me because of it. Thank you for all your help and support in transforming that belief. We have had an increase of about 37% in our sales numbers this year over last and I'm positive it's due to having the Sandler Selling System in place.

– John Schwaderer • Operations Manager
High Country Window and Door

Not only is our team energized and booking more orders, we can show true ROI and continue to beat our competition as a direct benefit of learning the Sandler Selling System.

– Jay Batista • Vice President, Sales
VCI Solutions

The Sandler Selling System enabled us to gain a competitive sales advantage over other companies that were still using "traditional" sales techniques. The Sandler approach to cold calls, voice mail, finding pain and the psychology of "closing" were instrumental in helping us exceed our sales goals. Sandler is far and away better than any other training system I have ever encountered.

– Jay Fraze • Director of Sales and Board of Directors
Cherry Creek Chamber of Commerce

Thank you Sandler! Your system has helped us improve revenue production by 25% in 6 months!

– Roger Elizondo • Center Director
LasikPlus Vision Center of River Oaks/Sugar Land

This stuff works! It has given our sales team the tools they need to know where they are in the sales process and effectively control the process. This is the "lean" process for sales. It really cuts the waste out of selling time and energy!

– Blain Tiffany • President
Castle Metals Plate

THE SANDLER® RULES

Forty-Nine Timeless Selling Principles ... And How to Apply Them

The most successful sales techniques ever revealed based on the rules developed by David H. Sandler, creator of the Sandler Selling System.

Adapted by

DAVID MATTSON

PEGASUS
Media World

Publisher
Pegasus Media World
PO Box 7816
Beverly Hills, CA 90212

For further information please visit www.sandler.com or call: 1-800-638-5686

The Sandler Rules: Forty-Nine Timeless Selling Principles ... And How to Apply Them
© 2009 Sandler Systems, Inc.
ISBN, print ed. 978-0-9822554-8-3

Cover design: James Kim
Interior design: Jonathan Siegel

First Printing: 2009

Publisher's Cataloging-in-Publication

Mattson, David
The Sandler Rules: Forty-Nine Timeless Selling Principles ... And How to
Apply Them / David Mattson. – 1st ed.
p. cm.
Includes index.
"The most successful sales techniques ever revealed, based on the rules
developed by David H. Sandler, creator of the Sandler Selling System."
LCCN 2008942411
ISBN-13: 978-0-9822554-8-3
ISBN-10: 0-9822554-8-9

1. Selling.   I. Sandler, David H. II. Title.

HF5438.25.M382 2009   658.85

QBI08-600343

About Dave Mattson
CEO, Sandler Systems, Inc.

Dave Mattson is the CEO and a partner at Sandler Systems, Inc., an international training and consulting organization headquartered in the United States. Since 1986, he has been a trainer and business consultant for management, sales, interpersonal communication, corporate team building and strategic planning throughout the United States and Europe. Clients often describe his creative enthusiasm, problem solving and curriculum design as particular strengths that he uses to increase their companies' productivity and efficiency.

An early lesson for Dave in the sales process was the law of cause and effect: *If one works hard, then he will be rewarded. If one prospects, then his funnel will be full. If one has goals, then he will be farther ahead than if he had none.* The impact of cause and effect holds true in all aspects of life, especially our selling life. This approach dovetailed with the concepts and methodology that are the foundation of Sandler Training, and are succinctly expressed through the Sandler Rules, a series of selling rules created by David Sandler to guide the behaviors and interactions of salespeople in buying-selling situations. When it came to selling, the Sandler Rules seemed clear as day – "if *this* happens, then you do *that* …"

In 1986, Dave met the founder of Sandler Training, David H. Sandler, and fell in love with his training material. In 1988, he went to work for Mr. Sandler, and was eventually chosen to lead the company.

Dave conducts training sessions and seminars around the world. He has noticed countless times that, as soon as he says to the class, "Here's a Sandler Rule," participants listen with undivided attention, and that the Sandler Rules are easily recalled as long as 15 years after the training.

Dedication

To David H. Sandler, whose profound understanding of human nature and keen devotion to the selling profession enabled him to not only create the most effective selling process, but also to raise the level of professionalism for salespeople throughout the world.

Acknowledgements

Thank you to the following individuals, without whose help this book would not have been possible. To the Sandler trainers around the world who give life and passion to David Sandler's work, and who have helped take the Sandler organization to heights and dimensions that David Sandler himself never dreamed possible. To the home office team, for your hard work and dedication to making Sandler the most innovative and effective training and consulting company in the world. To my partner, Bruce Seidman, for sharing a common vision for Sandler Training. To Howard Goldstein, for your devotion to the integrity of David Sandler's message and working tirelessly on this project. And a special thanks to my family for their unconditional love and support.

TABLE OF CONTENTS

RULE

PART THREE:
COURSE-CORRECT

139

REMIND YOURSELF OF WHAT'S EASY TO FORGET.

EPILOGUE:
SOME FINAL THOUGHTS ON GOOD TIMES, BAD TIMES, AND THE BEHAVIORS BEHIND THEM

INDEX

PROLOGUE

THE MAN
BEHIND THE RULES

David Sandler didn't start out to build a global sales training organization, become a renowned sales trainer, or even become a salesperson. His introduction to the business arena came as a youngster, working summers in his family's snack foods distributor business. In his early twenties, he was a route driver calling on small grocery stores. At the age of thirty-six, he was the president of the company and, in his words, "on easy street."

Then his world crumbled.

After losing a proxy fight with his business partner, he lost the job that should have lasted his lifetime–along with the cars, the perks, and the country club membership that came with it.

With a family to provide for and a mortgage to pay, David went to work for a former competitor in the snack industry. To supplement his income, he took a part-time sales job with a distributor of motivational programs–tapes, records, and books. Any "selling" he had performed in the snack food business was essentially order-taking – servicing the account and occasionally letting people know about a new product or promotion. Selling motivational materials was foreign to him, but he figured he could probably pull it off. The company had a training program that was supposed to ensure his success; he started looking it over.

David diligently studied the training materials. He learned how to make a sales presentation, how to handle objections, and how to close. Working nights and weekends, he called on anyone who would listen to him. He didn't enjoy selling – actually, he hated it – but he needed the money, and he stuck with it.

Despite the put-offs and the rejections, he made countless cold calls; thanks to sheer determination, his work paid off. Before long, he was the company's only productive salesperson. In fact, he was the only remaining salesperson at the company. Less than a year after entering the world of professional sales as a part-time salesperson, David bought the distributorship.

Now he had another decision to make – whether to give up the security of his daytime job. To succeed in selling, he knew he'd have to be fully committed to the profession. He resigned from the snack business, never to return. He was now back in business for himself.

David learned a lot about the traditional ways of selling – what worked and what didn't. He learned a lot about himself – what he liked about selling, what he didn't like about selling, and how to motivate himself (or trap himself) into doing the things he didn't like to do.

David then set out to learn as much as he possibly could about human behavior … to better understand why prospects act the way they do, as well as what really motivates them to buy. This phase of his career laid the groundwork for the training system that bears his name … and produced his most widely quoted "breakthrough" observation: "People make buying decisions emotionally … and they justify those decisions intellectually."

Today, just about everyone in sales acknowledges the wisdom of that observation, and accepts that a) the prospect must be emotionally involved in the sale, and b) some kind of pain must effect the prospect on an emotional level for the sale to move forward.

What does any of that mean to you? What are you supposed to do to elicit the emotion? What does this kind of high-minded talk have to do with the job of selling?

The answers lie in a theory of psychology and psychotherapy known as Transactional Analysis – T-A, for short. T-A was developed by a psychiatrist named Eric Berne in the late 1950s. When David Sandler developed the Sandler Selling System® methodology, he used T-A as his human relations model, and used it to back up his explanations of the reasons buyers and sellers act the way they do. T-A is the foundation for the rules in this book and the entire Sandler approach, so it is worthwhile to summarize T-A briefly before we begin.

WHAT T-A SAYS ABOUT HUMAN BEHAVIOR

T-A theory defines three ego states that influence our behavior – the *Parent,* the *Adult,* and the *Child.*

The *Parent* ego state is that part of us where information is stored about such things as what is good and bad, right and wrong, appropriate and inappropriate.

The *Adult* ego state is the logical, analytical, rational part of our behavioral framework. It weighs the pros and the cons, the pluses and the minuses, the upsides and the downsides.

The *Child* is the *emotional* part of our makeup. This is where feelings are stored. *Read this part twice:* T-A theorizes that by the time we are six years old, we have experienced and stored a wide range of emotions – emotions that influence us throughout the balance of our lives. That goes for sellers, buyers, and everyone else.

The *Child* is where many of our decisions originate – not just buying decisions, but all kinds of decisions. The *Child* is that little six year old in us who, feeling a particular emotion at a particular time, says, "I want this," "I want to do that." Or perhaps: "I don't want this," and "I don't want to do that."

Sandler's rules were revolutionary to the selling world because they recognized that the *Child* started the process. The *Parent* wasn't going to judge whether a purchase was appropriate or not, and the *Adult* wasn't going to weigh the pluses and minuses of the purchase or the pros and cons of a particular vendor. There had to be some emotion driving the process. Sandler saw that the *Parent* and the *Adult* weren't going to get involved until the *Child* said, "I want it."

Getting the *Child* to express that desire is the objective of the critical phase of the relationship that we now call the *Pain* step in the Sandler Selling System. (By the way, if you want to learn more about the full Sandler Selling System and the various steps it incorporates, please drop us a line at info@sandler.com or visit us at www.sandler.com.)

Getting prospects emotionally involved in the sale doesn't necessarily mean they have to *be* emotional – unhappy, angry, distraught, fearful, or feeling any other specific emotion. Nor does it mean that the prospect has to *express* an emotion. It simply means that the prospect's inner *Child* is saying, "I want it."

Why is your prospect's *Child* saying, "I want it?" Perhaps it's because you helped him discover something he didn't know before he met you. Maybe you helped him see his situation from a different perspective, and uncovered some doubt about an existing strategy. Perhaps you helped him focus on the real root cause of his problem. Perhaps his *Child* is saying, "I want to know what this person knows" or "I want what this person has to offer." Whatever the motivation, you will not close a sale unless the emotional component of your prospect's identity – the *Child* – first signs off on the deal.

Sandler also recognized that simply "hooking" the prospect's *Child* wasn't the answer. This leads to the second part of his most famous observation. Look at it again: "People make buying decisions emotionally … *and justify those decisions intellectually.*"

At some point, the prospect's *Parent* is going to ask questions like, "Do you really need this?" and "Are you sure you're not acting too impulsively?"

What's more, the prospect's *Adult* is going to ask questions like, "Can you afford this?" and "Are there better alternatives?"

As a result of these questions, the prospect may very well come to have second thoughts – and if we don't play our cards right, the sale that was "in the bag" may be put on hold.

That's why the Sandler Selling System has *Budget* and *Decision* steps – to satisfy the intellectual aspect of the decision. From the salesperson's perspective, these are qualifying steps. From the prospect's perspective, though, these steps provide an opportunity for the *Parent* and *Adult* to be involved in the process. The *Parent* and the *Adult* get to specify under what conditions the buying decision will be deemed appropriate and logically sound.

It was David Sandler's genius that caused him to discover these basic principles and codify them. Armed with the information that we are talking, not to one prospect, but to three – the *Child,* the *Parent,* and the *Adult,* we can plan accordingly. We can present our product or service in such a manner that the *Parent* says, "Okay, this seems to be the right thing to do. You have my permission." We can present our product or service in such a way that the *Adult* says, "After weighing all the information, this makes good sense. Go ahead." And we can present our product or service in such a way that the *Child* says, "Yes, that's what I want."

Selling to three people, when it might look like you're only selling to one, takes practice. The forty-nine selling rules that are set out briefly here – the Sandler® Rules – have been field-tested now for over three decades. They are what you should practice if you want to exploit what David Sandler discovered, via Transactional Analysis and his own personal experience, to be true about the human condition.

The Sandler Rules are relevant to all salespeople, and indeed to any student of human decision-making. Some of what you read here will give you insights about the prospect. Some of what you encounter will give you insights about yourself. *All of it must be reinforced over time.*

Full disclosure: If you are a sales professional, the very *best* way to reinforce what you are about to learn will be to work with a Sandler trainer over an extended period. If you can't do that right now ... this book can hold you over until you can.

David Sandler died far too young, and it remains a deep loss for all of us who knew him, all of us whose lives he touched directly or indirectly, that he himself did not oversee a project such as this one. Since the matter has been ordained as it has, please credit him with what is worthwhile here – and hold me to account for what may be deficient in the recording of his ideas. They are his ideas, and not mine. My goal in compiling this book has been simply to preserve the core elements of what I believe to be the soundest selling philosophy available from any source.

See whether you agree. Put the Sandler Rules to work. Don't just read the book once. Read its principles and employ its concepts until they become second nature to you. If David Sandler spent decades refining these rules, and he did, it is realistic to assume that you, too, will need some time – time to make the Sandler Rules something you *do*, not just something you know.

– David Mattson

PART ONE:

LEARN THE CORE CONCEPTS

Use the first six rules to transform your selling process.

SANDLER
RULE #1

YOU HAVE TO LEARN TO FAIL, TO WIN

Have you ever lost a sale – and felt like a personal failure?

- It's OK to fail.

- You as a person are not a failure.

- There is the REAL-you vs. the ROLE-you.

Failure is part of the human condition. Everybody fails at something. People who achieve a great deal fail at many things.

You can choose to regard failures as negative experiences – defeats, losses, setbacks. Or you can choose to regard failures as positive experiences – opportunities for you to learn what not to do, what needs to be changed, and what needs to be fixed. Failure can accelerate your success ... if and only if you take the time to extract clear lessons from your failures, and then apply those lessons to your next endeavor.

> YOU EITHER CHOOSE TO LEARN SOMETHING FROM THE EXPERIENCE OF FAILING - OR YOU CHOOSE NOT TO DRAW ANY LESSON AT ALL FROM YOUR MISTAKES.

Recognizing failure as a potential positive experience gives you a new freedom – the freedom to try new things, be more creative, and stretch outside your comfort zone. If you don't achieve the results you seek, ask yourself, "What did I learn from this?"

Of course, accepting this concept *intellectually* is one thing. Dealing with failure *emotionally* is another matter entirely. Before you can learn *from* your failures, you must learn to *fail*. And, in order to do that, you must understand failure and put it in its proper perspective.

THE REAL-YOU VS. THE ROLE-YOU

When you fail to accomplish something, YOU are not a failure. You – a person with intrinsic worth – did not fail. Instead, it was your attempt – your action plan, strategy, or technique – that failed. There is a difference between the REAL-you and the ROLE-you.

The REAL-you is defined by your self-identity ... your sense of self-worth.

The ROLE-you is defined by your performance in a role – brother, sister, spouse, parent, little league coach, or salesperson.

You may not be a particularly skilled little league coach, for instance, but that doesn't devalue your self-worth – the REAL-you. It only means that there is room for improvement in your little league coaching skills.

The same goes for your salesperson role. You'll fail to schedule appointments with some people. You'll fail to close sales with others. The failure is not a reflection of the REAL-you, only the ROLE-you. These "failures" are nothing more than an indication that there is room for improvement in your "salesperson skills."

You must learn *not* to take role-failures personally. An unsuccessful attempt to obtain an appointment or close a sale is just that – an unsuccessful attempt. It has nothing to do with your personal worth. Your personal worth is still intact!

If there is a lesson to be learned from the failed attempt, identify it and apply it to subsequent attempts. End of story!

You will know when you have learned to *fail* in a way that supports *winning* – as opposed to failing in a way that you take personally – because you will start thinking about "failure" differently. When you begin to look forward to the lessons from "failures," because you know those lesson will lead you to future "wins," you will be on the right track.

TEST YOUR
UNDERSTANDING

WHAT ARE THE POSITIVE
RESULTS OF FAILURE?

SEE ANSWER BELOW.

BEHAVIORS

REFLECT ON A RECENT "FAILURE" ... AND IDENTIFY THREE LESSONS YOU LEARNED FROM THAT EXPERIENCE. THEN IDENTIFY A CURRENT OR UPCOMING OPPORTUNITY WHERE YOU CAN APPLY THOSE LESSONS.

Answer: You learn a lesson about what not to do, which can stimulate creativity and accelerate your learning curve. Accepting "failure" as normal gives you the freedom to try new things without putting your self-esteem at risk.

SANDLER
RULE #2

DON'T SPILL YOUR
CANDY IN THE LOBBY

Have you ever shared too much information, too soon?

- Have you taken a *trip* at the movies?
- Get the prospect to talk.
- Save your knowledge and expertise.

You stood in line for twenty-five minutes to buy your ticket. You spent another eight minutes in line at the candy counter. Finally, with two minutes to spare, clutching your $4 box of candy, which you just couldn't wait to open, disaster struck. You headed for the theater doors all ready to find a good seat and munch your way through the movie – but not three feet from the door, you stumbled on a ripple in the carpet. As you lurched forward, so did the contents of your candy box.

Now you are recovering, as gracefully as possible, from your fall. You make your way to a seat and settle in. But, with most of your candy on the floor out in the lobby, the movie experience just won't be the same. If you had

> DON'T GIVE AWAY
> TOO MUCH,
> TOO SOON.

only waited a few more minutes before opening that box!

What does a spilled box of candy have to do with sales? Everything! When you go on a sales call, you bring with you a "box of candy." Your box of candy is your knowledge and expertise. Many salespeople are eager to open the box as soon as possible and let all the candy spill out. As soon as the prospect expresses a concern that can be addressed by the salesperson's product or service, the salesperson moves into presentation mode, highlighting key features and benefits, and even including a third-party testimonial or two for good measure. "Candy," "candy," and more "candy!"

There's a time for all that "candy," of course: during a formal presentation, demonstration, or proposal review. And even then, you only want to focus on the elements that specifically pertain to issues and concerns you and your prospect have previously identified – together.

KEEP THE "CANDY" IN THE BOX

During the initial phase of a sales call – the fact-finding phase – the "candy" must remain in the box. Your task now is to ask questions and gather the information you need to fully understand the prospect's situation. Your task is to take notes on the problems to be solved or goals to be achieved. Your task is to determine if your product or service is truly a best fit for the situation. Your task is *not* to dump "candy" on the floor! That leads, all too often, to an unfortunate state of affairs: You tell the prospect all about your products and services. After the sales call, you walk out bewildered: "Why didn't I get an order? I told them every reason why they should buy – but nothing happened!"

If you're routinely dropping off information, proposals, and marketing materials without really understanding your customer's buying motives – you are making a habit out of spilling your candy in the lobby. Ask yourself: Once they have your information and pricing, do they really need you anymore? Your prospects wouldn't shop your information to your competitors – would they?

Instead, gather enough facts to qualify the opportunity fully. If you get far enough along in the development cycle to make a presentation, then you can open the candy box.

Yes – you can and should help the prospect. The best way to help early on in the game, however, is by asking questions. Say as little as possible and get the prospect to talk as much as possible. Your job is to get information, not give it. Save your goodies for later.

TEST YOUR UNDERSTANDING

WHAT IS THE DANGER OF SPILLING YOUR CANDY IN THE LOBBY?

SEE ANSWER BELOW.

BEHAVIORS

IDENTIFY THE SPECIFIC TIMES DURING SALES CALLS WHERE YOU ARE LIKELY TO BE TOO EAGER TO SHARE INFORMATION. ASK YOURSELF: WHY DO I WANT TO SHARE THIS INFORMATION? IS IT, PERHAPS, THE RESULT OF A DESIRE TO ESTABLISH CREDIBILITY OR DISPLAY EXPERTISE?

FOR EACH INSTANCE YOU IDENTIFY, DEVELOP SPECIFIC QUESTIONS YOU COULD ASK TO DETERMINE WHETHER THE INFORMATION YOU ARE NOW "SPILLING" IS ACTUALLY RELEVANT AND OF INTEREST TO THE PROSPECT.

Answer: By spilling your candy early in the sales development cycle, you run the risk of revealing aspects of your product or service the prospect has no interest in or doesn't understand. In either case, you give the prospect reasons at the very beginning of the process to say "no" to your offer or, even worse, express the desire to "think it over."

SANDLER
RULE #3

NO MUTUAL MYSTIFICATION

Have you ever heard what you wanted to hear from the prospect – and lost the deal as a result?

- Do you have "happy ears?"
- Confirm what everyone understands.
- Confirm what's happening next.

"I'M EAGER TO SEE WHAT YOU CAN DO FOR US!"

Bill is contacted by the CFO of ABC Company, whose employee benefits insurance business Bill has been pursuing for three years. The CFO says that he is eager to see what Bill's company can do for him, and requests a quote ASAP. This is music to Bill's ears!

Bill believes his persistence has finally paid off. He immediately contacts ABC's Human Resources department to obtain the reams of employee data he will need to develop a proposal. And he gets to work.

Has Bill's persistence finally paid off? Or is the CFO simply in search of a competitive quote he can use as a bargaining chip with his current broker?

"COME ON IN!"

This morning, Tom made contact by phone with a prospect who was quite enthusiastic about his call. The prospect was eager to find out how Tom's marketing company could help her promote the grand opening of her new store. She briefly described some of her objectives and enthusiastically granted him an appointment.

Tom now believes he is going to meet with her and ask scores of questions to further define the scope of the event, discover her expectations, and identify the availability of resources. The prospect, on the other hand, thinks Tom is coming in to make a presentation.

The "crystal ball of sales" predicts that Tom has an uncomfortable meeting in his future.

"MONEY IS NO OBJECT!"

During a meeting, Suzanne asked her prospect directly whether there was funding in place for the consulting project they were discussing. The prospect replied, "Money is no object." Suzanne certainly didn't imagine that the prospect's comment gave her carte blanche, but she did feel relief that she wasn't going to be constrained by financial pressures as she began to develop the project.

> DO BOTH SIDES KNOW WHAT'S HAPPENING NEXT?

Should Suzanne feel comfortable? Did the prospect mean that funds were, for all practical purposes, unlimited? Or did he mean that money was "no object" because *there wasn't any money available?* (Yes, there are prospects who will give you answers like this.)

Sometimes, salespeople have "happy ears." They tend to hear what they want to hear. What they believe they heard through those happy ears may not reflect the real intent of what the prospect said.

It is the salesperson's responsibility to:

• Determine the prospect's intentions and expectations.
• Help the prospect be more specific and define any ambiguous terms or phrases that may be misinterpreted.
• Tie up any loose ends.
• Make sure all parties to a conversation or meeting are "in sync" with what just transpired … and what is supposed to happen next.

Make it a practice to recap the conversation after interactions with prospects or clients. Say something like this: "Let me quickly recap what we discussed to make sure we're all on the same page and we didn't leave anything out." Then review the conversation in detail, and conclude by asking something like this: "Does anyone have anything to add … did I miss anything or misunderstand anything?"

Eliminating *Mutual Mystification* today reduces the opportunity for misunderstandings and unfulfilled expectations tomorrow.

TEST YOUR UNDERSTANDING

WHAT IS THE "HAPPY EARS" PROBLEM?

SEE ANSWER BELOW.

BEHAVIORS

IDENTIFY ONE OR MORE INSTANCES WHERE YOU WERE MISLED BY THE "HAPPY EARS" SYNDROME. FOR EACH INSTANCE, DEVELOP THREE OR MORE QUESTIONS YOU COULD HAVE ASKED TO CLARIFY OR CONFIRM WHAT YOU BELIEVED YOU HEARD.

Answer: Sometimes, salespeople hear what they want to hear. That is, they interpret a prospect's words to mean something more favorable to their cause than a logical and unemotional interpretation would indicate.

SANDLER
RULE #4

A DECISION NOT TO MAKE A DECISION IS A DECISION

Have you ever had a prospect tell you, "I need to think it over?"

- What does "let me think about it" mean?
- Figure out what's going on.
- Give people permission to say "No."

Nancy made a follow-up call to a prospect who had previously requested some information from her. Her intention was to have a brief conversation, qualify the opportunity, and schedule an appointment, if that was appropriate. The prospect revealed that he'd received and read the information – and was "very interested." But, he added, he needed a bit more time to "digest" what she'd sent him before deciding on an appointment.

Nancy agreed to get back to him in a week.

The procurement committee said that they were ready to make a decision and granted Rich ninety minutes to present his proposal. Rich explained the details supporting each point of his proposal. He addressed each and every committee member's concerns. He answered all of the questions that came up, and received what he believed to be a nod of approval after each answer. He asked if there was anything else they needed to see or hear from him. They all said "No" – and they all commended him on the thoroughness of his presentation. You already know where this is leading, don't you?

Rich didn't. He felt quite positive about his presentation. Confidently, he asked for their decision. After some mumbling amongst themselves, they announced that they needed some time to "think it over" and promised to get in touch with Rich within a week or so, when things calmed down.

Do you suppose Nancy obtained the appointment? After all, the prospect was "very interested." What about Rich? Did he get the sale? They all said he'd been very thorough, and they all promised to "think it over."

When you request an appointment, attempt to close a sale, or ask a prospect or customer to take any other course of action, you are asking for a decision – a commitment to do something *or* not do something. In short, you are asking for a "Yes" or a "No." You are not after anything in between those alternatives.

When a prospect decides not to decide – when a prospect gives you a "think-it-over," in whatever form that takes – the odds are high that you have been treated to a convenient disguise for "No."

> UNCOVER THE TRUTH, EVEN IF IT'S NOT SOMETHING YOU WANT TO HEAR.

Prospects may rationalize the (apparent) indecision as a means of "protecting" you – letting you down slowly and not hurting your feelings. More likely, the prospect is protecting *himself* from having to explain a "No" decision. Offering you a "think-it-over" is usually an effective strategy for avoiding a potentially uncomfortable social situation.

When asking prospects or customers for a decision, let them know in advance that a "Yes" is desirable, but a "No" is OK. That's right; a "No" is OK. (See also Rule #43: *You don't learn how to win by getting a "Yes" – you learn how to win by getting a "No."*)

When you give prospects permission to say "No," and make it very clear that "No" is OK, they are less inclined to disguise what they tell you with some form of "think-it-over."

When interacting with prospects and clients, your objective is to uncover the truth, even if it's not something you want to hear. After all, if the answer is going to be "No" – the prospect *isn't* going to grant you an appointment, your customer isn't going to buy the latest promotion, the prospect isn't going to become your next customer – wouldn't you want to know sooner, rather than later?

TEST YOUR UNDERSTANDING

WHAT MUST YOU DO IF
YOU WISH TO DENY
YOUR PROSPECTS
THE LUXURY OF SAYING
"LET ME THINK ABOUT IT?"

SEE ANSWER BELOW.

BEHAVIORS

REFLECT ON THE LAST THREE "THINK-IT-OVER" SITUATIONS YOU HAVE ENCOUNTERED. DETERMINE THREE THINGS YOU COULD HAVE DONE, EITHER PRIOR TO THE EVENT OR AT THE TIME OF THE PROSPECT'S INDECISION, WHICH WOULD HAVE ALLOWED YOU TO OBTAIN A CLEAR YES-OR-NO DECISION.

Answer: You must be comfortable telling your prospect that it's OK to say "No." You must also be comfortable hearing and accepting "No."

SANDLER
RULE #5

NEVER ANSWER AN UNASKED QUESTION

Have you ever introduced a topic the prospect wasn't expecting – and stopped a deal in its tracks?

- Avoid the salesperson's nightmare.
- Learn how to blow a deal.
- See the dangers of "You're probably wondering ..."

Don invested three months developing a comprehensive IT solution for a prospective client. He effectively orchestrated the interactions between the prospect company's buying team and his sales team. The project objectives were defined with laser-like precision. All the potential implementation roadblocks had been identified and resolved. Timelines and deadlines had been established. Don and his team had generated a complete and compelling proposal. He was absolutely confident he would win the business – and he had every right to be confident.

At the proposal presentation, Don first reviewed the project objectives and requirements and reconfirmed that they were the elements on which the buying

> DURING THE PRESENTATION, FOCUS ON THE ISSUES YOU AND THE PROSPECT HAVE DISCUSSED – NOTHING ELSE.

decision would be made. Don then covered each phase of the project – point by point. After each point, he asked the buying team members if they were 100 percent comfortable with what he presented. They affirmed that they were. Don reviewed the financial arrangements to which they had previously agreed. No problems there. Don was entering the home stretch, confident that he would close the sale.

Don wasn't quite finished with his presentation when the buying-team leader interrupted, "Don, we don't need to see any more. We're ready to move ahead with the project. We'd like you to get things going as soon as possible. Let's complete the paperwork."

Even before Don could breathe a sigh of relief and pull the contract out of his portfolio, a member of his tech support sales team killed the deal.

The tech guy blurted out, "You should know that there's an update coming for the database program. We're just about finished beta testing it. The final version should be ready in about 60 days."

A strange silence fell over the room.

THE UNASKED QUESTION

Of course, in the tech-support person's mind, the prospect buying team *should have* asked about software updates. Even though they didn't ask, he felt it was important to provide an answer.

The tech-support person was not, strictly speaking, a salesperson. But there are plenty of salespeople who have answered similarly inopportune unasked questions at similarly critical moments.

You can guess what happened. The tech support member's answer to the unasked question derailed what was shaping up to be a "slam-dunk," and quickly transformed it into a disaster. The prospect decided to hold off signing the contract … and ended up working with someone else.

Why did the deal die? In Don's world, software updates are a fact of life, something that's routinely handled with little or no inconvenience to the client. The fact that Don didn't mention it, and his team member felt compelled to bring it up at the last moment, cast some suspicion on the "slam-dunk" proposal.

The objective of a presentation is to present the aspects of your product or service that address the issues and concerns previously identified … and nothing more. This is not the time to introduce new elements. If, during a presentation, you've ever said something like, "You're probably wondering how we would …" and then gave an explanation about some new element that is supposed to add value to your offering, or entice your prospect to buy, then you're guilty of answering an unasked question. If the prospect had been "wondering" about it, he would have asked!

TEST YOUR UNDERSTANDING

INCLUDING "ADDED VALUE" ELEMENTS IN YOUR PRESENTATION NOT PREVIOUSLY DISCUSSED WITH THE PROSPECT CAN:

☐ A) DEFLECT ATTENTION AND INTEREST AWAY FROM THE CENTRAL ISSUES OF THE PRESENTATION.

☐ B) CONFUSE THE PROSPECT AND GIVE HIM A REASON TO POSTPONE MAKING A BUYING DECISION.

☐ C) ESTABLISH REASONS FOR THE PROSPECT NOT TO BUY FROM YOU.

☐ D) ALL OF THE ABOVE.

SEE ANSWER BELOW.

Answer: All of the above.

BEHAVIORS

IDENTIFY THOSE ASPECTS OF YOUR PRODUCT OR SERVICE THAT YOU ROUTINELY INCLUDE IN YOUR PRESENTATIONS TO DEMONSTRATE "ADDED VALUE," WHETHER THE PROSPECT HAS ASKED ABOUT THEM OR NOT. NEXT, IDENTIFY WHERE IN THE SELLING PROCESS, PRIOR TO THE PRESENTATION, YOU CAN INTRODUCE THOSE ITEMS IN A WAY THAT "TESTS THE WATERS" AND DETERMINE THEIR RELEVANCE TO THE PROSPECT'S SITUATION — AND THE PROSPECT'S LEVEL OF INTEREST IN DISCUSSING THEM.

SANDLER
RULE #6

DON'T BUY BACK TOMORROW THE PRODUCT OR SERVICE YOU SOLD TODAY

Have you ever had a buyer change his mind
after committing to the sale?

- Deal with buyer's remorse.

- "Get the order and get out" is not the answer.

- Give the prospect the chance to back out.

Sometimes a salesperson obtains a buying decision from a prospect one day only to have the prospect call the next day – before the paperwork has even been processed – instructing that the sale be put on hold, or worse, cancelled altogether. Perhaps this has happened to you.

What went wrong? Obviously, the prospect had second thoughts. Perhaps a concern or unanswered question from an earlier stage of the selling process resurfaced. Or maybe someone in the prospect's world demanded that he work with another provider – or no provider at all.

Of course, these sudden reversals are no salesperson's idea of a good time. In some circles, salespeople of years past came up with an inventive way to defend themselves against such backtracking:

> THERE'S AN IDEAL WAY TO OVERCOME "BUYER'S REMORSE."

the "get the order and get out" strategy. Under this strategy, you were supposed to close the sale, get the order signed, and get back to the office as quickly as possible to have it processed. Then it was someone's responsibility to ensure that the product was shipped or the service implemented as quickly as possible – before the customer had the opportunity to back out!

ANOTHER WAY

While that kind of behavior on the part of selling organizations is not as prevalent today as it once was, it's worth understanding. The "get the order and get out" strategy was designed to circumvent the effects of buyer's remorse – the prospect having doubts about the buying decision he made and then backing out of the deal. Trapping the customer into the sale may ensure one sale, but it will likely destroy the chances of a long-term relationship.

Rather than attempting to trap the buyer into accepting a deal, a better strategy is to make sure the prospect is 100 percent comfortable with the proposed sale *before* "signing on the dotted line" – and make absolutely sure there are no reasons to back out.

How do you accomplish that? Rather than reviewing all of the positives – the benefits and advantages of the product or service – in an attempt to reinforce the prospect's decision to move forward with the sale, you should actually give the prospect a *chance* to back out before "sealing" the deal. You read right: Give the prospect a chance to back out! Encourage him to take a hard look at his decision and make sure he has no doubts. If there were any elements of the deal that represented compromises, bring them up and make sure the prospect is now completely comfortable with them.

This strategy accomplishes three things. First, it enhances your credibility. Only someone who is extremely confident in the product or service and the structure of the sale would encourage a prospective customer to reexamine his decision. Second, this strategy gives the prospective customer a chance to reconfirm the choice. If there are second thoughts, the prospect has an opportunity to express them in a no-pressure environment. Third, if the prospective customer *does* have doubts, you can address them while you are still face-to-face, which is usually far more effective, and far easier, than trying to deal with them over the phone.

Here's an example of what it might sound like:

You: Bill, I look forward to working with you and your company. My technical people can meet with your development team next week. Before you sign the contract and we schedule that meeting, let me ask you a question. What could come up that would cause you to call me and tell me to put the contract on hold?

Bill: I can't think of a thing.

You: And you're absolutely sure a six-week implementation schedule rather than a four-week schedule, as you had hoped, isn't going to be a problem?

Bill: I'm certain. We're eager to get this project off the ground but two weeks longer for implementation is perfectly acceptable. Let's get it going.

Giving the prospect a chance to back out while you're still face-to-face to deal with his concerns or doubt is much better than receiving a voice mail message that says, "Hold the order. I'll call you next week to explain."

TEST YOUR UNDERSTANDING

WHAT ARE THREE BENEFITS OF DEALING WITH BUYER'S REMORSE IMMEDIATELY AFTER OBTAINING THE PROSPECT'S COMMITMENT TO BUY?

SEE ANSWER BELOW.

BEHAVIORS

IDENTIFY THREE SELLING SITUATIONS WHERE SOME FORM OF BUYER'S REMORSE EMERGED AFTER YOU "CLOSED" THE SALE. FOR EACH, IDENTIFY SOMETHING YOU COULD HAVE SAID, ASKED OR DONE TO IDENTIFY THE POTENTIAL PROBLEM AND DEAL WITH IT AT THE CONCLUSION OF EACH PRESENTATIONS.

Answer: 1. Reinforces your credibility. 2. Provides you with an opportunity to address any unresolved issue that may have been temporarily put aside – and forgotten. 3. Gives the prospect an opportunity to deal with any potential second thoughts and reconfirm his buying decision ... while he is still talking to you.

PART TWO:

EXECUTE

Do what works.

SANDLER
RULE #7

YOU NEVER HAVE TO LIKE PROSPECTING, YOU JUST HAVE TO DO IT

Have you ever put off your prospecting tasks
... and faced an income crisis as a result?

- Focus on the end result.

- Prospecting is a selection process.

- Cast your net.

The salesperson who claims to "like" making cold calls hasn't made any.

How can anyone "like" a process that produces such an arena for rejection? When salespeople say they like prospecting, what they may mean is this: "I don't mind paying the price of prospecting to reach my objectives." Many salespeople haven't reached that stage. If you're still at the stage where prospecting means dialing numbers and hoping the line is busy ... or driving around the block for two hours so you can build up your nerve to call on a complete stranger, don't worry. You're OK. You just haven't learned to focus on the end result ... instead you are focused on what you have to do to get the end result.

FIND THE PROSPECT!

Prospecting is simply the act of finding prospects – those people who need your product or service – while they are hiding in a sea of suspects. You must keep your focus on that goal: finding prospects. You can't let your attention become diverted by the many suspects you will encounter along the way. When you're prospecting, you're like the Coast Guard's Search and Rescue team, looking for a small raft of shipwreck survivors in a vast ocean. The work may be long and tedious, but the goal is certainly worthwhile and rewarding.

Of course, along the way, the Coast Guard team may encounter all kinds of interesting crafts – colorful sailboats, magnificent yachts, even an ocean liner or two – in their search for the survivors' raft. That doesn't mean they call off the search! Similarly, you will encounter many interesting suspects, but you never want to call off your search for the prospect who needs you. Keep your focus on those people who qualify as prospects. The goal is not to *convert* suspects to prospects, any more than it is to convert an ocean liner to a life raft. Your goal is simply to weed out the suspects who don't qualify as prospects as quickly and efficiently as possible.

You will encounter many more people who don't need your product or service (or won't admit to the need) than people who do. There will be many more people who won't want to talk with you than people who will. This is the nature of the job of selling, not something to regret.

Admittedly, cold calling is not the most glorious of all selling activities. That may be because it takes place at the beginning of the selling cycle, with the payoff for the effort still comparatively far off in the future. However, whether it is glamorous or not, it is a strategically essential activity that gives you control over, and adds predictability to, your selling efforts.

Cold calling, like other prospecting activities, is a *selection* activity – it's all about separating prospects from suspects, nothing more and nothing less. When it's time to prospect (and it usually is) think of yourself as being like the fisherman who, upon pulling up the net, must sort through the catch and throw back all the fish that are too small. Some days, you'll throw back many small fish. Other days you'll throw back only a few. The one thing you *must* do, however, and do with a consistency that borders on obsession, is cast your net! After all, that's your job!

TEST YOUR UNDERSTANDING

TRUE OR FALSE:
YOU SHOULD MAKE
A HABIT OF FOCUSING
YOUR ATTENTION ON
THE SHORT-TERM,
POTENTIALLY EMOTIONALLY
CHARGED ASPECTS
OF PROSPECTING.

SEE ANSWER BELOW.

Answer: False. If you focus on the emotionally charged, "undesirable" aspects of prospecting – the inevitable turn downs and rejections that are part of the process and nothing more – rather than on the more distant end results of the process, you set yourself up for frustration and disappointment.

BEHAVIORS

IF YOU TEND TO VIEW PROSPECTING AS AN UNDESIRABLE ACTIVITY AND YOUR OUTLOOK ABOUT IT HAS BEEN LESS THAN POSITIVE, WRITE A DETAILED DESCRIPTION OF THE BENEFICIAL OUTCOMES YOU HAVE RECEIVED IN THE PAST FROM "CASTING YOUR NET." WHAT NEW CLIENTS DID YOU IDENTIFY? WHAT WAS THE TOTAL DOLLAR VALUE OF SALES OBTAINED FROM THEM? WHAT REFFERALS DID YOU UNCOVER?

CONSIDERING THE BENEFICIAL OUTCOMES DESCRIBED, GENERATE THREE OR MORE ENDINGS TO THE FOLLOWING STATEMENT. PROSPECTING IS A DESIRABLE ACTIVITY BECAUSE:

SANDLER
RULE #8

WHEN PROSPECTING,
GO FOR THE APPOINTMENT

Have you ever tried to deliver a "sales pitch" to someone you just met?

- Prospecting is not selling.
- Don't second guess.
- Use a model for your prospecting calls.

Prospecting is a set of activities for identifying prospective users of your product or service – nothing more and nothing less.

Prospecting takes place before, and leads to, the selling process. It is *not* selling. It is not a time to discuss features and benefits, technical aspects, advantages and disadvantages, pricing, delivery, or any other "selling" points about your product or service.

Whether you are contacting prospects by phone, calling on them at their place of business, or having a conversation during a business function, the two-fold goal is the same: Engage the potential prospects (*suspects*) in a conversation about your product or service, and determine whether they have any interest. If they do, propose an appointment for further discussion at a later time. These discussions can take place face-to-face or over the phone.

If there is sufficient interest … just schedule the appointment. Any "selling" will take place *after the prospect has been qualified.*

TAKE THE PRESSURE OFF

PROSPECTING IS
NOT SELLING.
SO DON'T SELL
— JUST SET THE
APPOINTMENT.

"Going for the appointment" takes the pressure off the salesperson and the prospect. The salesperson doesn't have to second-guess which aspects of his product or service are appropriate to bring up. And, because he's not facing a premature "sales pitch," the prospect doesn't have to put up a defensive wall of stalls and objections.

Here is an example of what setting an appointment by phone might sound like.

You: Hello, this is Marcia Powers. Who is your chief executive, please? (Wait for response.) Would you be nice enough to put me through to Mr. Smith? Thank you.

You: Mr. Smith, this is Marcia Powers of Evolutionary Technologies. Have I caught you at a bad time?

Mr. Smith: No.

You: (If there's pushback:) I can understand if you're busy. Let me ask you this, when's a better time for us to talk?

You: (If there's no pushback:) Mr. Smith, this is a prospecting call. I bet you don't like getting them, and I know I don't like making them. But the reason I'm calling is that we just performed a service for Jones Industries that improved their compliance with EPA regulators – while reducing their operating costs. With their OK and in the best interests of your industry, we can share much of this information with you at no obligation to your company. I don't know whether or not your company would be too big or too small for this service, but I believe it would make sense for us to get together to see why Jones Industries was so enthusiastic. Are you open-minded to taking a look at how it might apply to your company?

TEST YOUR UNDERSTANDING

WHY IS PROSPECTING NOT TO BE CONFUSED WITH SELLING?

SEE ANSWER BELOW.

Answer: Prospecting is the act of identifying those individuals who have enough of an interest in your product or service to have a more substantial conversation with you. Any selling activities – such as qualifying the opportunity, or discussing the various aspects of your product or service – must take place during subsequent conversations.

BEHAVIORS

Examine your prospecting approach and identify any "sales pitch" elements — features, functions, and advantages of your product, service, or company — that might cause a prospect to raise his or her defenses. For example: "We're the largest supplier of ...," "We manufacture the most reliable ..." and "For over twenty years we've provided the most extensive assortment of ..." These statements signal an imminent sales pitch to the prospect.

Convert your features and advantages to beneficial outcomes that are more likely to arouse the prospect's curiosity and spark a conversation. For example: "Other electrical contractors in your region rely on us to provide them with an extensive assortment of ..." or "Several members of your trade association have increased membership by an average of 14 percent with our help."

SANDLER
RULE #9

EVERY UNSUCCESSFUL PROSPECTING CALL EARNS COMPOUND INTEREST

Are you using your experience on past calls to improve the next call?

- You will have more unsuccessful calls than successful calls.
- What put-offs do you get?
- Learn over time.

You can't win them all – at least, not when you're prospecting. Not everyone you call on will need or want your product or service. Some will need what you have to offer, but not now. Others won't know that they need what you're selling, even though you're certain that they do need you.

The reality is that you are likely to have more unsuccessful calls – calls ending with turn-downs and put-offs – than successful ones. But you can learn something from the unsuccessful calls that will contribute to a win down the road. (See Rule #1: *You Have to Learn to Fail, to Win.*)

> EVERY PROSPECTING CALL CAN IMPROVE THE NEXT CALL.

For instance, suppose you are receiving the same put-offs time and again – the pre-programmed responses prospects use to fend off salespeople who sell what you're selling. After just a few such calls, you can prepare better by developing your own "preemptive strike."

Suppose, for example, that you sell employee benefits packages. Rather than start your conversation with a business owner with a request to review the current program, or with statements about the advantages your company can provide, both of which will probably lead to a put-off, you might try the following:

You: If you are like most business owners, as soon as I mention employee benefits programs, you're going to tell me, "We're already working with someone" or "We're covered." Would you be willing to put those on the shelf for two minutes while I explain why I called – and then decide if there is a reason to talk further?

By bringing up the put-off first, you diminish its impact and let the prospect know that it isn't going to work with you – you're not afraid of it. This approach distinguishes you from all the other salespeople who found themselves trying to "overcome" the put-off. Notice that this strategy is based on a lesson you learned in a previous call.

WHAT'S THE LESSON?

Commit to learning a lesson on every call and applying it to subsequent calls. These don't have to be earth-shattering lessons. They should be something you could do more effectively … or something unproductive that you can avoid doing. The lessons learned, even from those "unsuccessful" calls, compound over time and lead you to big rewards.

TEST YOUR UNDERSTANDING

WHAT ARE THREE ADVANTAGES OF BRINGING UP OBJECTIONS ON A PROSPECTING CALL BEFORE YOUR PROSPECT HAS AN OPPORTUNITY TO VOICE THEM?

SEE ANSWER BELOW.

BEHAVIORS

IDENTIFY THE OBJECTIONS YOU HEAR MOST OFTEN FROM DECISION MAKERS WHEN PROSPECTING. DEVELOP A PROSPECTING CALL OPENING THAT 1) PREEMPTS THESE OBJECTIONS AND 2) ENCOURAGES A CONVERSATION.

Answer: 1. Weakens the objection. 2. Sets you apart from most other salespeople. 3. Eliminates the need to "arm-wrestle" with the prospect over the objection.

SANDLER
RULE #10

DEVELOP A PROSPECTING AWARENESS

*Are you missing out on conversations
with people who could have bought from you?*

- Who are suspects and prospects?
- Could the person next to you on the bus become a prospect?
- Play the "Duck Pond" game.

As you may have gathered by now, a *suspect* is someone you might be able to sell to, but have not yet connected with in any way. A *prospect* is someone you connect with who is interested in talking with you further about what you sell. Here's the thing: The person sitting next to you on the airport shuttle bus counts as a suspect. That person *could* turn out to be a prospect ... but you won't know until you start a conversation.

IN SEARCH OF THE RIGHT DUCK

Are you familiar with the "Duck Pond" game? You can find it at most carnivals. There's a group of plastic ducks floating in a large tub. For the price of a ticket, you get to choose a duck. On the bottom of the duck is a number that corresponds to the prize you "win." Most often, the prize isn't worth the price of the ticket. But if you continue playing the game, find a way to keep track of the ducks you've already chosen, and bring just a little bit of luck to the game, you may find the duck with the number that corresponds to the big stuffed animal that's actually worth *more* than the price of your tickets.

> SUSPECTS WHO
> ARE ABOUT
> TO TURN INTO
> PROSPECTS LOOK
> A WHOLE LOT LIKE
> SUSPECTS WHO
> ARE ABOUT TO SAY
> "NO."

Prospecting is a similar "game." This game, like all games, has an objective: Finding, within a large group of *suspects*, a smaller group of *prospects*. Prospects, unlike suspects, have given you evidence that they are capable of graduating to the level of customer. Finding prospects is the first goal in the game of sales; finding prospects is what can help you win the big prize.

Just as the plastic ducks in the tub all look alike, suspects who are about to turn into prospects are hard to distinguish from suspects who won't. You must examine each suspect to determine whether he qualifies as a prospect. As you engage in your prospecting activities and work your way through the group of suspects, looking for prospects, you will of course, encounter many more people who don't qualify as prospects than people who do. This situation can be very frustrating ... *until* you recognize that sorting through suspects is just part of the process – a process that leads to a big payoff.

In essence, prospecting is not any different than picking up a duck, examining the number, and then, if it doesn't hold the number to the big prize, putting it back and choosing another duck. If you're making telephone cold calls, that means simply picking up the phone again and dialing the next number!

Prospecting is not limited to picking up the telephone, of course. In fact, you have opportunities for prospecting in virtually any social situation. At Sandler Training, we teach salespeople to observe what we call the "three foot rule," meaning that anyone you could reach out and touch represents a potential opportunity for business. Again: You will never know for sure whether you are three feet away from a prospect … until you strike up a conversation!

The suspect you start chatting with on the bus may not qualify as a prospect … today. But she may reveal some information that gives you reason to call on her in the future when she *is* likely to qualify as a prospect. She may know of others who are more likely to be prospects. Each attempt brings you one step closer to the "big prize." Each suspect you connect with may be able to point you in the direction of a prospect, thereby accelerating your process.

The more ducks you pick up – the more aware you become of a suspect's ability to turn into a prospect or lead you to one – and the more eager you will be to pick up the next duck!

TEST YOUR UNDERSTANDING

WHAT DISTINGUISHES PROSPECTS FROM SUSPECTS?

SEE ANSWER BELOW.

BEHAVIORS

IDENTIFY AT LEAST FIVE DIFFERENT OPPORTUNITIES YOU HAVE TO "REACH OUT AND TOUCH" A SUSPECT, INITIATE CONVERSATIONS, AND DETERMINE IF THEY QUALIFY AS A PROSPECT. DEVELOP AND APPROPRIATE CONVERSATIONAL OPENER FOR EACH OPPORTUNITY.

Answer: A suspect may have a casual interest in your product or service. A prospect is someone who has enough of an interest to be willing to have an in-depth conversation about it.

SANDLER
RULE #11

MONEY DOES GROW ON TREES

Are you getting your fair share of referrals?

- Grow your network, so you don't have to "start from scratch."

- Add a branch.

- Water your tree.

Let's face it. When it comes to developing new business, it's no fun to have to start the selling cycle all over again, time after time. Fortunately, there is a better way.

Draw a straight line vertically down the center of a piece of paper. Connect that line with a horizontal line at the bottom of the page. Now, every time you sell a prospect, extend a branch from the vertical line. This is your referral tree. That branch you just added is a sign of sales growth. It can generate branches of its own!

If you're "working hard," as opposed to "working smart," (see Rule #34: *Work Smart, Not Hard.*), you will have a tree that looks like a trunk with mostly dead branches on it. So what would "working smart" look like when it comes to referrals?

The salesperson who "works smart" uses the referred lead to sustain and support new growth on the tree. Every time this salesperson makes a sale, she asks for a referral. She then can work her way from "cool" to "warm," establishing a relationship with this new prospect – a relationship based, initially, on the work she's done in the past with her customer. When she eventually sells this new prospect, she adds on to the branch of the customer who gave her the referral – and asks the new customer for a referral!

You can actually see it grow. Someone who's "working hard" – but generating few deals and few referrals – will have a referral tree that looks like something you'd see in the dead of winter. Someone who's "working smart" will enjoy consistent referral growth with every new sale – and start more new business relationships by means of a referral.

> YOU DON'T HAVE TO "START FROM SCRATCH" EVERY TIME.

Amateur salespeople hate the thought of prospecting because it means they have to start "cold" every time. Professionals who know how to "work smart" are experts at working the *referral tree*. They spend more time beginning their sales cycle with leads that are "cool," "warm," or even "hot!"

There is an added bonus to consider here. Even "cool" leads you generate from your referral tree are much, much easier calls to make than classic "cold" calls! If you think for just a moment, you'll realize how true this is. Would you rather talk to John Smith's *gatekeeper* with the name of someone who has asked you to get in touch with John, or *without* that name to mention? Of course, you want to be able to say something like this: "I'm calling for John Smith; Michael Jones asked me to call. Can you put me through to him, please?" John Smith is very likely to take that call!

So here's a guaranteed money-maker for your referral tree: Each time you make a sale, write a letter or send an e-mail to *all* of the customers on the branch that led you to that sale, thanking the person who gave you the referral! Water your referral tree by letting your customers know you appreciate them. Money does grow on trees!

```
┌─────────────────────────────────────────┐
│                                           │
│           TEST YOUR                       │
│        UNDERSTANDING                      │
│                                           │
│                                           │
│      WHAT ARE TWO ADVANTAGES              │
│          OF CULTIVATING                   │
│       A REFERRAL "FOREST?"                │
│                                           │
└─────────────────────────────────────────┘
```

SEE ANSWER BELOW.

BEHAVIORS

IDENTIFY SIX CLIENTS WITH WHOM YOU CAN BEGIN TO PLANT A REFERRAL "FOREST." SET DATES TO MEET WITH THEM — AND PLANT MONEY TREES.

Answer: 1. You don't have to start your prospecting efforts over and over again by making cold calls. 2. Prospects are more likely to take your calls and engage in a conversation.

SANDLER
RULE #12

ANSWER EVERY QUESTION WITH A QUESTION

*Have you ever answered a prospect's question
– and wished you hadn't?*

- Find the intent behind the prospect's question.

- DON'T answer automatically.

- You put stress on yourself when you make a habit
  of answering "directly."

Hey, what does this rule mean?
Why are you asking?
Isn't that obvious?
What do you mean by "obvious?"
Why won't you answer my question?
What makes you think I won't answer your question?
Aren't you avoiding answering my question right now?
Am I?

No, you shouldn't use this rule as an excuse to play silly games with the prospect. But behind the rule is a valid concept: Prospects usually don't ask the real question up-front. (See Rule #38: *The Problem the Prospect*

Brings You Is Never the Real Problem.) Instead, prospects ask "smoke-screen" questions that *hide* the real question and its intent. By answering these "smoke-screen" questions directly, instead of posing questions of your own, you run the risk of boxing yourself in.

WHAT IS THE PROSPECT'S QUESTION SUPPOSED TO ACCOMPLISH?

Here's an example. Bruce represents a marketing and public relations firm. He is meeting with the owner of a new restaurant to discuss an advertising campaign. The owner asks, "How much experience does your firm have creating advertising campaigns for restaurants?" Bruce's company has a substantial amount of experience with restaurants. So Bruce answers confidently: "Actually, we have quite a bit of experience with restaurants. We've created a number of very successful campaigns." His prospect then replies, "Well, I hope you're not planning on presenting me with some recycled ideas."

> DON'T BOX YOURSELF IN. FIND OUT THE INTENT OF THE QUESTION YOU'VE BEEN ASKED.

Bruce might recover, but look at all the pressure he put on himself by not finding out the intent of his prospect's question before answering. Had he discovered the real intent of the restaurant owner's question, Bruce could have provided an answer more appropriate to the *real* question. Let's give Bruce another chance. Suppose he answered the restaurant owner's smoke-screen question with a question.

Owner: How much experience does your firm have creating advertising campaigns for restaurants?

Bruce: That's a very good question. And, you're asking because …?

Owner: We're a unique restaurant – our menu is unique, our venue is unique – and we want to make sure that any advertising reflects that uniqueness.

Bruce: That makes perfect sense. Probably the first thing I should tell you is that we recognize that each project has a distinctive set of variables. Each project has to support the client's message with the right theme, the right copy, and the right images. We know that no two restaurants are the same, and that's why no two campaigns are the same.

Bruce never answered the owner's smoke-screen question; instead, he answered the real question.

In the example, Bruce got to the real question very quickly. Sometimes, it takes two or three questions to discover the prospect's real question.

Also, notice that Bruce didn't simply "fire back" his response. First, he commended the owner for asking a good question, and then he gave a thoughtful, appropriate answer.

Are there times when you should just answer the prospect's question and not respond with a question? Of course – when you are certain that the answer can help you, or at least can't hurt you. For example, if your prospect asks, "What time is it?" responding with "Good question ... why do you ask?" will most likely get you a funny look from your prospect.

TEST YOUR UNDERSTANDING

WHAT IS THE BIGGEST DANGER OF OFFERING DIRECT ANSWERS TO YOUR PROSPECT'S QUESTIONS?

SEE ANSWER BELOW.

BEHAVIORS

RECALL THREE SELLING SITUATIONS WHERE YOU PROVIDED A PROSPECT WITH A DETAILED ANSWER TO WHAT TURNED OUT TO BE A "SMOKE-SCREEN" QUESTION. FORMULATE RESPONSES THAT WOULD HAVE HELPED YOU UNCOVER THE REAL INTENT OF YOUR PROSPECTS' QUESTIONS.

Answer: Unless you understand the intent of the question, i.e., the "real" question, you run the risk of providing an answer that boxes you into an unfavorable selling position.

SANDLER
RULE #13

NO MIND READING

Have you ever made an ASSUMPTION about a prospect that turned out to be unrealistic?

- Don't assume facts not in evidence.

- Don't *mis*read between the lines.

- Ask what the prospect means.

One prospect says, "This looks very good. I think there's an excellent chance we'll do business together." The salesperson thinks, "I've got one!"

Another prospect says, "We were hoping for a shorter delivery time." The salesperson thinks, "I'll have to push this through as a rush order if I want to win this sale."

Each salesperson is guilty of *mind reading* – assuming facts not in evidence and *mis*reading between the lines.

In the first example, exactly what does *an excellent chance* mean? We have no idea. We need to find out. Similarly, was the second prospect's *hope* for a shorter delivery time actually a *demand*, or was it merely out-loud thinking about the potential need to adjust a schedule? There is no way to tell without asking for clarification.

When a prospect uses words or phrases that are vague, ask for an explanation. For instance, it would be appropriate for the salesperson to ask the first prospect what "excellent chance"

GET THE FACTS.

really means. A first step to determining the meaning behind the second prospect's comment might be, "And you're telling me that because …?"

Don't jump to conclusions. Get the facts.

"YOU MUST BE TELLING ME THAT FOR A REASON."

When Bob's prospect said, *"We're already working with a supplier,"* Bob responded with a long list of the benefits of buying from his company rather than from other suppliers. Most of the items on that list were totally irrelevant to his prospect's world.

A better dialogue for Bob might have been this one:

Prospect: We're already working with a supplier.
Bob: You must be telling me that for a reason.
Prospect: Well, we've been doing business with them for several years.
Bob: Which means …?
Prospect: We've been pleased with their service.
Bob: And …?
Prospect: And, there would have to be a good reason to switch.
Bob: Like …?
Prospect: Well, I'm not sure. I suppose quality control would be a factor, we've had a higher rate of flawed product shipped to us than the CEO is looking for.

Now Bob has something to talk about! By *responding* to the prospect's statement with a statement or question, Bob was able to avoid mind reading and uncover the intent of the original statement – the prospect's respect for a vendor relationship of several years – and eventually discovered an opening for a discussion.

No one can know what a prospect is thinking. Isn't it worth a few questions to find out?

(See also Rule #12, *Answer Every Question with a Question,* and Rule #38, *The Problem the Prospect Brings You Is Never the Real Problem.*)

TEST YOUR UNDERSTANDING

WHY MIGHT VETERAN SALESPEOPLE BE MORE LIKELY TO VIOLATE THIS RULE THAN THOSE WHO ARE NEW TO THE SALES PROFESSION?

SEE ANSWER BELOW.

BEHAVIORS

IDENTIFY TWO "STALL" OR "OBJECTION" STATEMENTS LIKE, "YOUR PRICE IS TOO HIGH," OR "YOUR COMPANY IS NOT ON OUR APPROVED VENDOR LIST." WRITE OUT TWO OR THREE PLAUSIBLE REASONS WHY A PROSPECT WOULD MAKE EACH STATEMENT. THEN DEVELOP A FEW QUESTIONS YOU COULD ASK TO HELP UNCOVER THE TRUE MEANING OF EACH STATEMENT.

Answer: Veteran salespeople have more experiences to call on and relate to a current situation, making it easier for them to jump to a conclusion before discovering the relevant facts about a prospect.

SANDLER
RULE #14

A PROSPECT WHO IS LISTENING IS NO PROSPECT AT ALL

Have you ever talked yourself out of a sale?

- Are you "selling" ... or "telling?"

- Highlight a potential problem.

- Get the prospect talking about it ... then shut up!

YAKKETY YAK

Here's a reliable selling principle: During any given sales meeting, the prospect should be mostly talking and the salesperson mostly listening. This principle is especially important during initial sales meetings.

David Sandler suggested that the prospect should be talking about 70 percent of the time. Typically, however, the opposite occurs. The salesperson feels compelled to talk about as many features, benefits, and unique selling points of his product or service as time permits ... in an attempt to "capture the prospect's interest."

If the prospect merely wants a rundown on the technical details of your product or service, he can simply visit your web site or read your marketing brochure. Investing time to meet with you would not be necessary.

"SELLING" – OR "TELLING?"

"Selling" is not about "telling." It's about helping the prospect relate your product or service to the satisfaction of his wants and needs. It's also about helping him discover needs of which he was previously unaware. How do you accomplish this? By asking thought-provoking questions and then listening … *really* listening.

Let's examine the difference. Telling sounds like this:

> "Our software analyzes warehousing and distribution costs in relation to regional sales patterns and identifies areas for cost saving. In more than 72 percent of the studies performed in the last 12 months, we've discovered typical savings of between 18 and 34 percent across a range of industries. Yakkety, yakkety reliable. Yakkety, yakkety return on investment. Yakkety, yakkety, 24/7 support."

Informative? To a degree. Thought provoking? Not particularly. You might as well hand the prospect a brochure and conduct a read-along!

Selling requires that you *engage* the prospect. You can educate and stimulate interest by means of a thought-provoking question much more effectively than you can by citing features and benefits. Here's an example of selling by means of an engaging question:

> YOU CAN OPEN YOUR EARS OR YOUR MOUTH, BUT NOT BOTH AT THE SAME TIME.

> "If you had a way to analyze your warehousing and handling costs, and compare them to your regional sales patterns so you could determine exactly how much money you're wasting now on excess capacity … what do you suppose you'd discover?"

Informative … and provocative! This kind of question engages the prospect by highlighting a specific potential problem – wasted investment in excess capacity. It stimulates a conversation about how useful it would be to be able to reliably analyze the situation. It gets the prospect talking.

When you get the prospect talking, shut your mouth; don't interrupt. You can open your ears or you can open your mouth, but you can't do both at the same time. Let the prospect finish, then ask questions or make comments. And, don't think about what you're going to say until the prospect has finished speaking. If you're thinking about what you are going to say … you're not listening!

You can lose a sale by talking too much. But you'll never, ever lose a sale by listening too much.

TEST YOUR UNDERSTANDING

WHY IS ASKING QUESTIONS A MORE EFFECTIVE APPROACH FOR OBTAINING YOUR PROSPECT'S ATTENTION AND INTEREST THAN TALKING ABOUT THE FEATURES AND ADVANTAGES OF YOUR PRODUCT OR SERVICE?

SEE ANSWER BELOW.

BEHAVIORS

FOR EACH OF THE IMPORTANT ASPECTS OF YOUR PRODUCT OR SERVICE, DEVELOP A THOUGHT-PROVOKING QUESTION THAT IS NOT ONLY INFORMATIVE BUT ALSO ENGAGES THE PROSPECT IN A CONVERSATION.

Answer: When you are presenting features and advantages, your prospect is in a passive mode – listening (you hope). When you ask thought-provoking questions that the prospect must answer, he is engaged in the interaction – no longer a spectator at the event.

SANDLER
RULE #15

THE BEST SALES PRESENTATION YOU WILL EVER GIVE, THE PROSPECT WILL NEVER SEE

Have you ever given a presentation that
left the prospect needing to "think about it?"

- Telling vs. selling, continued.

- Questions lead to discovery.

- "Typically, when I talk to people in your situation, the conversation revolves around A or B … "

Once, when this rule was presented during a training session, a participant raised his hand and asked, "Does that mean all presentations should be verbal … with no written materials or visuals?"

No. That's definitely not what this rule means!

What the rule is getting at is this: You should be helping the prospect *discover for himself* the best reasons to buy from you. How should that happen? Not by your telling and explaining, but by your *asking questions* that educate the prospect and lead him to that discovery.

Some people think the job of a presentation is to convince someone to buy. Is it? Here's a question to consider: Shouldn't the prospect's discovery of the very best reasons to buy from you happen *long before* you present?

The prospect is unlikely to *view* this process of identifying the best reasons to buy *by means of a question-and-answer dialogue* as a presentation. It is, however, more crucial to closing the sale than any dog-and-pony show you may put on – hence, the "presentation the prospect never sees."

Here's an example of the beginning of an "unseen" presentation:

Salesperson: Typically, when I discuss production efficiencies with owners of manufacturing facilities like yours, the conversation usually revolves around one of two areas – increasing production throughout without increasing reject rates, or decreasing production costs without sacrificing quality. Which, if either of those, matters most to you?

> HELP THE PROSPECT DISCOVER THE BEST REASONS TO BUY ... BEFORE YOU PRESENT.

Notice that the salesperson combined a story and a question, based on his own knowledge of the industry and the capabilities of his company. He focused on two specific areas of his company's expertise, and guided the conversation directly to those areas, and no others. Following the business owner's choice of Option A or Option B, the salesperson would then simply say, "Tell me about that." That approach causes the prospect to talk about an area of interest to him! Not just *any* area of interest, of course – one that is consistent with the capabilities of the salesperson's company!

During the ensuing "unseen" presentation, the salesperson would ask additional questions that continue to educate the prospect and focus on aspects of the service the salesperson's company provides.

Here are some examples:

Salesperson: If you analyzed the impact of your pre-production raw material staging procedures on production scheduling and, ultimately, production rates, what do you suppose you'd discover?

Salesperson: If your production team was able to integrate the de-burring and the final machining and polishing processes, how might that impact your production throughout?

Once you have identified the positive outcomes you can provide with your product or service, you may formulate questions to connect those outcomes — questions that enable your prospects to discover the benefits of those outcomes for themselves. When the prospect's discovery that it makes sense to work with you happens *before* the presentation, you will be selling at a whole new level — by making great "presentations" that your prospects never see.

TEST YOUR UNDERSTANDING

WHY DOESN'T THE PROSPECT "SEE" THE REAL PRESENTATION?

SEE ANSWER BELOW.

BEHAVIORS

GIVE A GREAT PRESENTATION ... BEFORE YOU GIVE A PRESENTATION. DEVELOP AT LEAST FIVE "TEST THE WATER" QUESTIONS TO MEASURE THE PROSPECT'S ACTUAL NEED OR DESIRE FOR THE OUTCOMES THAT YOUR PRODUCT OR SERVICE CAN DELIVER.

Answer: The prospect doesn't "see" the real presentation for four reasons: 1. It takes place early in the selling process, while the opportunity is still being defined. 2. It takes shape in the form of questions, rather than demonstrations and explanations. 3. It focuses on the prospect and his problems, challenges, or goals. 4. The prospect is so involved in his self interests that he doesn't perceive that the questions are leading him to conclusions.

SANDLER
RULE #16

NEVER ASK FOR THE ORDER – MAKE THE PROSPECT GIVE UP

Have you ever lost a deal – by trying to "close" it?

- Should you "always ask for the order?"
- Moving toward a mutual decision.
- The art is to get the prospect to "give up" on other options.

Most salespeople are taught to "always ask for the order." Asking for the order may be an acceptable strategy of last resort, but it really shouldn't be common practice. It tips the balance of equal business standing with your prospect. It puts him one notch up, and you one notch down.

If you have to *ask* for the order, then doing business together is not a "mutual" decision ... a mutual recognition of the benefit to forming a business relationship. Asking for the order is like asking for a favor. It leaves you beholden to your new client.

> IF YOU HAVE TO ASK FOR THE ORDER, THEN DOING BUSINESS IS NOT A MUTUAL DECISION.

"Make the prospect give up" *doesn't* mean "pressure the prospect into giving you the order." That, too, would upset the balance of equal business standing. What you are helping the prospect "give up" is his search for alternatives to deal with the concerns your product or service addresses. You are facilitating his decision to "give up" any lingering doubts about your product or service being the best fit for his situation.

Let's continue with the example from the previous rule. Take a look at how the dialogue might continue:

Salesperson: If your production team was able to integrate the de-burring and the final machining and polishing processes, how might that impact your production throughout?

Prospect: I'm sure it would have a positive impact, but to what degree … I don't know.

Salesperson: Would there be any value in conducting a study to determine the impact on production?

Prospect: I suppose so.

Salesperson: We can do that for you. Your investment would be nominal, and the report would provide you with the data you'd need to make a decision about reconfiguring the production line. Is that something you'd like me to do for you?

Prospect: It would be a good first step. How do we get started?

Notice that the salesperson was not pressuring for a "close" so much as continuing to engage the prospect with questions and guiding him to the sound decision to invest in an initial study. The final question – "How do we get started?" – was a request from one professional to another, not a plea from a subordinate to a superior. (The salesperson could also have asked, "What do we do now?")

Can it really be that easy? Yes … and no.

There are some prerequisites to making this kind of request work. You must develop some rapport and establish a degree of trust with your prospect that will allow him to have an open discussion with you. Also, you must be knowledgeable enough about your product and service to know the very best direction to guide your prospect.

Take stock. Identify the situations in which you are most often involved. Next, identify the solutions most appropriate to those situations. Then, develop the questions that will guide your prospects to those solutions. Practice, practice, practice … until you can ask your questions in a casual, matter-of-fact manner.

Finally – after you have done all that and laid the foundations of the relationship – ask the prospect what needs to happen next, as one colleague to another.

TEST YOUR UNDERSTANDING

WHAT PSYCHOLOGICAL IMPACT DOES ASKING FOR AN ORDER HAVE ON THE SALESPERSON?

SEE ANSWER BELOW.

BEHAVIORS

THINK OF AT LEAST TWO SITUATIONS WHERE YOU'VE ASKED FOR AN ORDER, RATHER THAN FINALIZING A NEW BUSINESS RELATIONSHIP AS ONE PEER TO ANOTHER. DEVELOP AND PRACTICE QUESTIONS THAT COULD HAVE GUIDED YOUR PROSPECTS TO THE CONCLUSION THAT WHAT YOU OFFERED WAS THE BEST SOLUTION FOR THE SITUATIONS THEY FACED.

Answer: It tips the balance of equal business standing in the wrong direction. It puts the prospect one notch up, in a position to grant the salesperson a "favor" – by giving him the order.

SANDLER
RULE #17

THE PROFESSIONAL DOES WHAT HE DID AS A DUMMY – ON PURPOSE

Do you routinely fill those uncomfortable silences?

- Is what you're about to do or say in your best interest?
- Wait out the silence.
- Sell like a doctor.

David Sandler always taught that you should never ask a question, make a statement, or behave in any way unless it is in your best interest to do so for the sale. He also taught that, as a general rule, a good sales discussion is one in which the prospect does the talking 70 percent of the time.

With both of these principles in mind, consider this question: *How* are you supposed to get your prospect to talk 70 percent of the time? Here's one answer: Know when to answer a question with a question (see Rule #12: *Answer every question with a question.*), and then stop talking. In other words, act like a dummy – on purpose.

You must learn to be brave enough to ask the "dummy question." Then *wait out the silence!*

For instance:

Prospect: I have to tell you: Your competition's price is a lot better than yours is.

You: Okay. Is it over? (Now wait out the silence!)

If remaining quiet in such a situation makes you feel uncomfortable or unprofessional, it shouldn't. Consider your relationship with your family doctor. Doctors are some of the best "answer a question with a question" practitioners on earth! Your doctor will often answer a question with a question – and when she does, you may be quite sure she will wait until she gets a straight answer from you before she recommends a course of treatment!

> RESTART THE SALE BY ASKING, "IS IT OVER?"

What happens when you arrive at your doctor's office complaining of a sore shoulder? After *listening* to your complaint, does the doctor simply accept your diagnosis? No. She asks you a series of questions ... and then waits for your response. It would be hard to have confidence in a doctor who asked her patient a question, then nervously filled in the silence by changing the subject before getting an answer.

For another example of this "dummy" technique, consider the old television show *Columbo*. Maybe you've seen the show. The rumpled detective is almost out the door ... then he stops for one more question, a "dumb" question that he apologizes for even asking. *He waits for the answer.* After a series of seemingly "dumb" questions, Columbo has the guilty party pretty much trapped. Another successful "dummy!"

"Is it over?" is a classic "dummy" question. (See also Rule #31 – *Close the Sale or Close the File.*) The answer to "Is it over?" will, if you wait for it, tell you precisely what is happening in the relationship, and will often lead you toward what you need next to regain your footing.

Sometimes, though, we ask the opposite of "dummy" questions, questions that are too smart for our own good. For instance: "Did you take into account all nine equipment categories covered by our service plan when you decided that we were more expensive than the competition?" It's easy for salespeople to go down this road when they've been selling for a while and know a whole lot about the features of their product or service. They're so proud of their knowledge that they can't wait to share it with anyone who will listen.

This brings us to one of the ironies of our profession. Back when we began our career, we asked prospects more "dumb" questions. Then, as the years went by, we got more and more certain that we knew what we were doing, and absorbed more product knowledge that we just knew we had to share with our prospects – somehow.

If we're not careful, our product knowledge, and our certainty that we know exactly what to say and do next, can overwhelm our own process and we may stop asking "dumb" questions. Typically, when this happens, we will start doing more of the talking in the sales meeting!

If we're lucky, we will learn to ask questions like a dummy again – and get back to the job of spending most of our time *listening* to the prospect.

That's the best way to make a medical diagnosis ... the best way to crack a tough criminal case ... and, eventually, the best way to forge a business relationship.

TEST YOUR UNDERSTANDING

WHY IS IT SMART TO ASK "DUMB" QUESTIONS?

SEE ANSWER BELOW.

BEHAVIORS

IDENTIFY THREE SALES SITUATIONS WHEN YOU MAY BE LIKELY TO TALK TOO MUCH. DEVELOP "DUMB" QUESTIONS YOU CAN ASK IN THOSE SITUATIONS TO SHIFT THE ATTENTION BACK TO PROSPECTS — AND ALLOW THEM TO EXPLAIN OR EXPAND ON THE SITUATIONS.

Answer: Asking "dumb" questions gives the prospect opportunities to talk – and explain and expand on his position. If you get the prospect talking, you'll be more likely to learn what you need to know to close the sale.

SANDLER
RULE #18

DON'T PAINT "SEAGULLS" IN YOUR PROSPECT'S PICTURE

Have you ever jumped in with a "great idea" that killed your sale?

- Whose painting is it, anyway?
- Ask questions that keep you safe.
- Let the prospect put the seagull in the picture.

Nancy was a second grader in the public school system. She had just completed painting a picture during art class. Considering her status as a "promising young artist," the picture of the house and the sun she created was quite good. It was obvious, however, that it was unbalanced, since everything was on the left side of the canvas.

> MAKE YOUR GREAT IDEA THE PROSPECT'S GREAT IDEA.

Nancy's teacher took a look at the picture and said, "Nancy, this is really a fine painting. However, it needs something on the right side." She then picked up a brush and painted a seagull in the upper right corner of Nancy's painting.

That evening, Nancy was quiet and withdrawn. At the dinner table, Nancy's father asked her what was wrong. She produced the picture, which was now folded up into a small square. Her father gently unfolded the picture and examined it. "Nancy, this is quite good," he told her.

"I especially like the seagull." Nancy fled the room in tears.

After her father learned that the teacher's seagull was the source of Nancy's problem, he complained to the art teacher, who, in her defense, cited her extensive credentials in the subject of art. The painting, she insisted, *did* need something on the right-hand side. Getting little satisfaction with the teacher, Nancy's father's next appointment was with the principal; the appointment that followed that was with his attorney.

One battle followed another and the conflict eventually led to a court hearing, complete with hours of testimony concerning the freedom of expression, the role of an educator, the nature of mental distress, etc. After listening intently to both sides, the judge asked Nancy why she had become so upset about the seagull. She replied, "Because I didn't see it there." Case closed, with the decision in favor of Nancy.

The point is, your prospect has a mental picture of his needs *before* you begin your sales interview. Every change or addition you make to the picture may cause the prospect to become just as uncomfortable as Nancy was. Every change you make to the "big picture" the prospect sees gives the prospect a reason to mistrust – or reject – your product or service. If a change or addition must be made to the prospect's picture in order for you to satisfy his requirements, you must find a way to propose that change indirectly. In other words, you must find a way to propose it that allows the *prospect* to discover the need and orchestrates the change.

How do you get the prospect to discover the need for a change? If you've paid attention to the last few rules, you've already figured it out: ask good questions. Appropriate questions will allow you to test the waters – without painting seagulls – and safely measure the prospect's reaction.

Here are some ways to structure your "test the waters" questions:

You: Do you suppose (s-e-a-g-u-l-l) would allow you to (satisfy your requirement) more effectively?

You: I don't suppose (s-e-a-g-u-l-l) would be of any value, would it?

You: You didn't mention (s-e-a-g-u-l-l), is that important?

You: It probably doesn't make any difference if we could (s-e-a-g-u-l-l) does it?

In each case, if the prospect were to respond positively, you would simply ask, "Why is that?" Now, the prospect must explain to you why he wants the *seagull*.

If the prospect were to respond negatively, your response would be, "I didn't think so." You're still safe! You've lived to fight another day. Maybe you can suggest the idea again from another vantage point.

If a seagull ends up in the prospect's picture, it should be because the prospect put it there.

TEST YOUR UNDERSTANDING

WHAT ARE "SEAGULLS" – AND WHY ARE THEY POTENTIALLY DANGEROUS?

SEE ANSWER BELOW.

BEHAVIORS

THINK OF A SPECIFIC TIME YOU ADDED A "SEAGULL" TO A PROSPECT'S PICTURE. WHAT WAS THE RESPONSE? NEXT, IDENTIFY THE "ADDED VALUE" ASPECTS OF YOUR PRODUCT OR SERVICE THAT TYPICALLY LIE OUTSIDE YOUR AVERAGE PROSPECT'S PERCEIVED NEED. FINALLY, DEVELOP SOME "TEST THE WATERS" QUESTIONS THAT WILL HELP YOU BRING THOSE ASPECTS TO LIGHT IN A SAFE MANNER.

Answer: "Seagulls" are aspects of your product or service for which the prospect has not yet expressed any need or interest. If you introduce seagulls before determining if the prospect has discovered the benefit of them, they provide the prospect with reasons to reject your offering.

SANDLER
RULE #19

NEVER HELP
THE PROSPECT END
THE INTERVIEW

Have you ever simply fled the scene of a meeting gone wrong?

- Don't fold up your tent just yet.
- Ask what you've said or done that was a problem.
- Let the prospect "dump."

> FIND OUT WHAT'S
> REALLY GOING ON.

From time to time, you'll find yourself dealing with prospects who are skeptical about the value of your product or service or your company's ability to "deliver the goods." For no apparent reason, you will get answers that are unresponsive, maybe even be a bit hostile. Perhaps they had a previous bad experience with your company, with another company that provides similar products or services, or with another salesperson who sells something completely different. Whatever the reason, the atmosphere can become uncomfortable. When this happens, should you simply "bail" on the meeting or discussion by saying, in essence, "I'm sorry I bothered you by coming in today?"

Even when you find yourself in a tense or awkward situation, you should not help the person end the meeting. Instead, make an effort to figure out what's going on. The prospect may have an agenda item that you don't know about, and a single "dumb" question, followed by silence, may help you uncover it. (See Rule #17, *The Professional Does What He Did As a Dummy – On Purpose.*)

If you're sensing that the prospect is skeptical, unenthused, even hostile, acknowledge it. Get it out in the open ... in a non-confrontational manner.

Here are a few examples:

You: Bill, you seem skeptical. It must be something I've said or done.

You: Bill, I'm picking up some uncertainty about what we're covering here. Is there something I've said or done you want to talk about?

You: Bill, I'm sensing some hostility. I suspect it's something I've said or done. Am I correct?

Get the awkwardness – or whatever strange emotion it is that you're picking up – out in the open. Put it on the table where the prospect can't possibly ignore it. Take responsibility for *raising* the issue, and a wonderful thing happens: you put the ball in the prospect's court. The prospect has to respond to your statement or question, and assume a share of the responsibility for *resolving* the situation. By allowing the prospect to "dump" about what you've "said or done" thus far, you clear the way for continuing the appointment in a better working atmosphere.

Try your best to figure out what's happening – *before* you volunteer to leave the premises. You may find an opening you hadn't seen earlier, and you'll definitely learn more about the prospect.

TEST YOUR
UNDERSTANDING

WHAT DO YOU HAVE TO
GAIN BY ACKNOWLEDGING
AND TAKING RESPONSIBILITY
FOR A MEETING THAT HAS
BECOME UNCOMFORTABLE
OR UNPRODUCTIVE?

SEE ANSWER BELOW.

BEHAVIORS

REFLECT ON TWO SALES MEETINGS THAT BECAME BOGGED DOWN OR OTHERWISE UNPRODUCTIVE. DEVELOP SOME QUESTIONS YOU CAN ASK IN FUTURE SITUATIONS THAT WILL BRING THE OBSTACLES TO THE FOREFRONT — AND ALLOW YOU TO TAKE RESPONSIBILITY FOR THEM.

Answer: Acknowledging the situation gets any problem out on the table where it can be dealt with. Taking responsibility for something you may have said or done to create the uncomfortable situation gives you the opportunity to engage the prospect, set things right, and continue developing the opportunity. If you are NOT the cause of the uncomfortable situation, the prospect will most likely bail you out and reveal what's really going on — valuable information you would never have obtained if you had simply ended the meeting.

88

SANDLER
RULE #20

THE BOTTOM LINE OF PROFESSIONAL SELLING IS GOING TO THE BANK

Do you know why you're showing up?

- Why are you doing all this?

- Salespeople keep score.

- What can you repeat?

What is your primary goal when you're calling on prospects?

Is it to develop a relationship? Generate interest for your product or service? Educate the prospect? Establish credibility? If you ask a dozen salespeople, you'll likely receive a dozen different answers. While each of these activities play *a part* in the development process, they are not, and should not become, the central focus of your call.

> REPEAT THE STEPS THAT ACTUALLY GET YOU CLOSER TO THE BANK.

The goal of calling on prospects, of course, is to close sales – that is, to *go to the bank*. Going to the bank is the *reason* you're doing what you're doing with the prospect.

In the sales game, the score is kept in dollars – sales completed, commissions earned, profits generated, and so forth. Salespeople are recognized and given awards for reaching or exceeding quota, for opening the most new accounts, for reaching a certain level of profitability, and so on. They are not given awards for "developing the warmest relationships," or for their "exemplary performance educating prospects." And they're certainly not given awards for "winning approval from others."

Invest your time in the activities that take you measurably closer to the bank. Don't spend a lot of time and energy on the activities that don't – like worrying about what the prospect thinks of you as a person.

Stay focused on qualifying opportunities up-front, using specific criteria as benchmarks. Stay focused on moving those qualified opportunities forward in a predefined manner – toward the bank. Don't waste time on vague "benchmarks" like *developing good relationships* in the hope that one day, one of those "relationships" will somehow be so "good" as to result in a sale. You can't measure "good relationship!" Ask yourself: *What has to happen in this relationship to get me closer to the bank?*

How much time should it take to develop and close an opportunity? Let history be your guide. For instance, if it typically takes 60 days to close a particular class of sale, and you're 120 days into the process, you probably went off track. If you have misjudged an opportunity – if it has stalled, dragging on without measurable progress – and if you have spent more time on it than is appropriate – let it go. Don't continue to "hang in there" because you and the prospect have a great "relationship," or because of the time you've already invested. If the prospect doesn't measure up, abandon the pursuit and redirect your energy on those opportunities that do.

Disqualified today doesn't mean disqualified forever. If there is a *clear understanding* – that is, an understanding that both sides can articulate – that the circumstances disqualifying the prospect today will change in some specific way in the future, resume your development activity at that time.

When you have specific criteria by which to judge an opportunity and when you make a commitment to *apply and abide* by those criteria, you improve your efficiency on each individual sale, and you expand your own potential for closing sales more quickly. With practice, you will learn to minimize the time spent with tire kickers and unqualified prospects. Your selling cycle will be shorter and your closing ratio will increase. You will find yourself going to the bank more quickly ... and more often.

TEST YOUR UNDERSTANDING

WHY IS "GOING TO THE BANK" THE KEY BENCHMARK FOR MEASURING SALES PERFORMANCE?

SEE ANSWER BELOW.

Answer: Ultimately, a sales organization's success (and survival) is determined by its bottom line profits. A healthy bottom line is a function of, among other things, profitable sales made in a timely manner – in other words, going to the bank. Sales opportunities that drag on longer than they should, or never get you to the bank at all, consume time and other resources ... and hurt the bottom line.

BEHAVIORS

IDENTIFY THREE ACTIVITIES YOU NOW JUSTIFY AS HELPING YOU "DEVELOP THE OPPORTUNITY" BUT THAT ACTUALLY DIVERT YOUR ATTENTION AND ENERGY FROM ACTIVITIES THAT WILL TAKE YOU TO THE BANK. NEXT, DETERMINE WHY YOU INVEST YOUR TIME IN THOSE ACTIVITIES. ARE YOU SIMPLY "WISHING AND HOPING" THE ACTIVITY WILL EVENTUALLY LEAD TO A SALE, OR ARE YOU AVOIDING OTHER ACTIVITIES THAT YOU CONSIDER LESS DESIRABLE? (PROSPECTING FOR NEW BUSINESS, SAY.) COMMIT TO ELIMINATING THOSE ACTIVITIES THAT ARE NOT INSTRUMENTAL TO HELPING YOU GO TO THE BANK MORE QUICKLY AND MORE FREQUENTLY. IDENTIFY WHAT YOU COULD AND SHOULD BE DOING IN PLACE OF THOSE ACTIVITIES.

S A N D L E R
R U L E # 2 1

S E L L   T O D A Y ,
E D U C A T E   T O M O R R O W

Have you ever lost a prospect's interest ... by talking too much about your product or service?

- You need a dialogue, not a monologue.

- Put your "educating" responsibilities to the side.

- Start with a question.

Many companies spend thousands of dollars producing PowerPoint™ presentations, flipcharts, and brochures in an attempt to provide sales aids for their salespeople. There is certainly nothing wrong with this type of material – but unfortunately most of it is not used productively. If you use this material during the period when you are still trying to identify the pain the person is experiencing, you run the risk of "spilling your candy in the lobby." (See Rule #2: *Don't Spill Your Candy in the Lobby*.)

> YOUR GOAL IS TO FIND OUT WHY, AND UNDER WHAT CIRCUMSTANCES, THE PROSPECT WOULD BUY FROM YOU.

The proper place for these aids is when you are delivering a presentation, and even then you should only be using those materials that help you demonstrate how your product or service can solve the specific needs and wants your prospect has painted for you.

Save the seminar on everything your product or service can do for later on. Right now, you're selling. That means your goal is to find out why, and under what circumstances, the prospect would buy from you.

Uncovering that information requires a dialogue, not a monologue. You must ask questions that will elicit the prospect's interests, concerns, and expectations. During your next initial interaction with a prospect, put your "educating" responsibilities to the side. Withhold your product knowledge and unique selling points. Instead, start with a question that will reveal the prospect's mindset about the acquisition of your product or service. Here is an example. Assume that you sell for a company that provides overseas shipping services:

> *You:* I suspect you have some specific concerns about your overseas shipments. Why don't you tell me what they are and then I'll do my best to address them?

Once the prospect reveals his concerns or interests, you can ask additional questions about their significance. The more questions you ask, the more the prospect talks – and the more you will learn about potential opportunities for positioning your product or service favorably.

TEST YOUR UNDERSTANDING

WHAT IS ONE DANGER OF ATTEMPTING TO EDUCATE YOUR PROSPECT TOO EARLY IN THE SELLING PROCESS?

SEE ANSWER BELOW.

BEHAVIORS

EXAMINE YOUR SALES DEVELOPMENT STRATEGIES WITH A CRITICAL EYE. DO YOU INVEST MORE OF YOUR TIME WITH A NEW PROSPECT ASKING QUESTIONS OR TELLING THE PROSPECT ABOUT YOUR COMPANY AND PRODUCT OR SERVICE? IF YOU DISCOVER THAT YOU ARE DOING A BIT TOO MUCH EDUCATING TOO EARLY, DEVELOP MORE QUALIFYING QUESTIONS. ASKING THESE QUESTIONS WILL ALLOW THE PROSPECT TO DESCRIBE CRITICAL NEEDS AND WANTS – AND HELP YOU IDENTIFY WHICH ASPECTS OF YOUR PRODUCT OR SERVICE THE PROSPECT WILL EVENTUALLY NEED TO BE EDUCATED ABOUT.

Answer: Attempting to educate the prospect about all of the features, functions, benefits, and advantages of your product or service early in the selling process shifts your focus from the more important first step of qualifying the prospect – determining why and under what circumstances the prospect would buy from you.

SANDLER
RULE #22

ONLY GIVE A PRESENTATION FOR THE "KILL"

Have you ever missed the "moment of truth" in your selling process?

- Prepare.

- Put the prospect "in your sights."

- Pull the trigger.

Through the trees, down the slope, across the ravine, up the opposite slope, and along the ridge – the hunter had been trekking through the brush since dawn. Finally, with the sun high in the sky, he had a clear shot at the trophy bull elk he had been tracking.

With the stock of his Weatherby Mark V rifle planted firmly against his shoulder, the hunter positioned the crosshairs of the scope for a perfect shot. Letting his breath out ever so slowly, he increased pressure on the trigger and then … then …

Well – after all that work, all those hours of preparation, *did* the hunter pull the trigger?

Of course he did. That was his goal from the outset. Everything he had done up to that point – choosing the hunt area, obtaining the appropriate license, researching the terrain, choosing the appropriate caliber rifle, practicing his marksmanship, sighting in the rifle scope — had prepared him for that one moment. His goal was to come home with a trophy elk … not a story about the trophy elk that got away.

You don't have to be a hunter, or even agree with the sport of hunting, to learn a valuable lesson from the story.

PREPARATION

When you deliver a presentation, you must be no less prepared than the hunter. You must have fully qualified the opportunity and decided for yourself that, in relation to the prospect's needs and goals and given the resources the prospect is willing and able to invest, your product or service really does provide a best-fit solution. You must have discovered the criteria by which your presentation will be judged — and decided that you can meet those criteria.

ARE YOU PREPARED TO CLOSE THE SALE WHEN THE PROSPECT IS "IN YOUR SIGHTS?"

And, most importantly, you must have secured a commitment from the prospect that he *will make a decision* at the conclusion of your presentation. Not only that, you must be resolute about obtaining that decision.

Without the preparation, without your own commitment for a decision, you may be able to get your prospect in your sights, but you won't be able to pull the trigger and bag your "trophy sale!" (See also Rule # 36: *Only Decision Makers Can Get Others to Make Decisions.*)

David Mattson

TEST YOUR UNDERSTANDING

WHAT DOES IT MEAN TO HAVE YOUR PROSPECT "IN YOUR SIGHTS?"

SEE ANSWER BELOW.

BEHAVIORS

CAREFULLY EXAMINE YOUR PRESENTATION PREPARATION ROUTINE, AND FIGURE OUT WHETHER YOU SET UP PRESENTATIONS IN A WAY THAT LEAVES YOU READY TO "PULL THE TRIGGER" ON A PROSPECT WHO IS CLEARLY "IN YOUR SIGHTS." IF YOU DISCOVER A PROBLEM, IDENTIFY THE INFORMATION THAT IS TYPICALLY MISSING, AND DEVELOP THE QUESTIONS YOU NEED TO ASK TO FILL IN THE BLANKS. THEN DETERMINE WHEN IN YOUR SELLING PROCESS YOU SHOULD ASK THOSE QUESTIONS.

Answer: Having the prospect "in your sights" means that you enter a presentation having fully qualified the prospect regarding the need for your product or service, the resources available to obtain it, the process for making a decision, and the elements on which your presentation will be judged. Most important of all, it means you have a commitment from the prospect to make a decision at the conclusion of your presentation.

99

SANDLER
RULE #23

THE WAY TO GET RID OF A BOMB IS TO DEFUSE IT BEFORE IT BLOWS UP

*Have you ever lost a sale because of a problem
you could have dealt with earlier on in the process?*

- If you know it's going to blow up in your face ... defuse it now.

- Figure out the problem sooner rather than later.

- Don't wait for the prospect to bring it up.

Sometimes, salespeople stress themselves out for no good reason. They sit around waiting for bombs to go off. Don't be one of those salespeople!

If you have the possibility of a recurring problem with your product or service, don't expose yourself to the stress of wondering when and how your prospect is going to lower the boom. Bring the issue up before the prospect does. Defuse it!

> BRING UP THE ISSUE BEFORE THE PROSPECT DOES.

Here's an example.

You: One of the problems we may have, Harry, assuming that we decide to do business together, is this. We don't provide local service. Is that going to be a problem?

Prospect: Yes, I'm afraid it may be.

You: Want to talk about that problem?

Prospect: Yes.

You: You start.

Bringing the problem up yourself makes it easier for you to handle the potential objection, rather than having to handle the problem while you're on the "defensive." This strategy can be applied to virtually any area of your sale (or post-sale) where you might reasonably expect to encounter a problem or disagreement: Financing, creditworthiness, delivery times, inventory status – you name it. If your experience tells you that there's the real possibility of you and the prospect experiencing a bump in the road, you should find a way to talk about it ahead of time.

Don't let the fear of "looking bad" or "losing momentum" with the prospect stop you from addressing the most important issues. You will, in fact, only look *more* professional in the prospect's eyes once you make it clear that you are willing to look around corners on his behalf. And if the obstacle is in fact going to keep the two of you from doing business together, you're better off knowing that now. (See also Rule #30: *You Can't Lose Anything You Don't Have.*)

TEST YOUR UNDERSTANDING

IN THE CONTEXT OF DEVELOPING A SELLING OPPORTUNITY, DEFINE "DEFUSING THE BOMB" – AND EXPLAIN THE BENEFIT OF THE STRATEGY.

SEE ANSWER BELOW.

BEHAVIORS

IDENTIFY THREE POTENTIAL "BOMBS" IN YOUR SALES ARENA – PROBLEMS OR ROADBLOCKS THAT TEND TO OCCUR WHEN YOU ARE DEVELOPING SELLING OPPORTUNITIES. DEVELOP SOME QUESTIONS YOU CAN ASK EARLY IN THE PROCESS TO DETERMINE THE LIKELIHOOD OF THE THREE IDENTIFIED PROBLEMS ARISING.

Answer: "Defusing the bomb" means bringing up a potential problem early in the selling process, before the prospect brings it up. The benefit of doing so is efficiency – dealing with potential deal-killers before you invest a great deal of time.

SANDLER
RULE #24

PRODUCT KNOWLEDGE
USED AT THE WRONG TIME
CAN BE INTIMIDATING

Have you ever overwhelmed a prospect with product knowledge?

- Does your prospect know what you're talking about?
- Are you intimidating prospects needlessly?
- Monitor facial and body cues.

> DON'T SABOTAGE THE SALE WITH YOUR EXPERTISE.

Your industry expertise and product knowledge can certainly be a professional asset – but you should also know that it can be intimidating to your prospects. If you use buzzwords, technical terms, or industry jargon early on in the selling process, before determining how familiar your prospect is with those terms, you run the risk of making your prospects uncomfortable. This is a major sin! *An uncomfortable prospect is unlikely to make emotional investments in your sales process.*

Prospects who don't understand what you are saying have two options.

Option one: They can be up-front and tell you that they simply couldn't make sense of some or all of what you said, and ask for an explanation. From your point of view, this is great when it happens, but be honest with yourself, this rarely happens. Why not? Because most people are simply uncomfortable asking for explanations. (This is particularly true when they're interacting with salespeople.)

Option two: They can remove the source of their discomfort: YOU! What would that sound like? Probably something like this:

Prospect: Well, Tom, I didn't realize that we would get into such detail today. I'm running a bit short of time. Why don't you leave the information and give me some time to review it, and then I'll get back to you.

Problem solved! No more discomfort.

Your product knowledge and expertise may enhance *your* confidence and make *you* feel more in control of your sales meetings. You should know, though, that flexing your intellectual muscles in front of your prospect may overwhelm him – especially when you're just starting your discussions.

During sales meetings, be sensitive to your prospect's facial expressions and body language. If you pick up any signal that you've made your prospect uncomfortable, back up. Say something like this:

You: Bill, I just ran through that information much too quickly. Let me back up.

Then review what you've just said using more appropriate language.

TEST YOUR UNDERSTANDING

WHAT'S ONE DANGER OF DISPLAYING LARGE AMOUNTS OF PRODUCT KNOWLEDGE TO YOUR PROSPECT DURING AN INITIAL APPOINTMENT?

SEE ANSWER BELOW.

BEHAVIORS

THINK CRITICALLY ABOUT YOUR INITIAL INTERACTIONS WITH PROSPECTIVE CLIENTS. IDENTIFY ANY INSTANCES WHERE YOU MAY TEND TO RELY ON PRODUCT-SPECIFIC KNOWLEDGE, TECHNICAL INFORMATION, OR INDUSTRY JARGON. DEVELOP ALTERNATIVE APPROACHES FOR DISCUSSING THOSE TOPICS. DON'T PRESUME THE PROSPECT HAS THE SAME DEGREE OF KNOWLEDGE AS YOU HAVE.

Answer: If you know more about your product than your prospect does, your display may make your prospect uncomfortable. And the easiest way for your prospect to deal with his discomfort is to remove its source – YOU.

SANDLER
RULE #25

WHEN YOU WANT TO KNOW THE FUTURE, BRING IT BACK TO THE PRESENT

Have you ever been asked to "get started" ...
before you closed the deal?

- "Do the groundwork."

- Play "Let's Pretend."

- What happens if ...?

> DON'T GET SET UP.

Many salespeople are asked by prospects to "do some groundwork" and "present the findings" at the next meeting. This "groundwork" might be compiling some preliminary figures, it might be performing a site survey, it might be creating a working diagram, it might be interviewing potential end users, or it might be doing some other initial work. The "findings" are meant to be an extensive analysis of everything that's been uncovered as a result of all that (unpaid) up-front work.

How often have *you* been in that situation?

Wouldn't you like to know what is likely to happen as a result of your efforts ... *before* investing your time and energy?

PLAY "LET'S PRETEND"

The Sandler "Let's Pretend" strategy will help you obtain the information you need. Here's what the request for "groundwork" from the prospect may sound like:

Prospect: I have to tell you, I'm impressed with what I've heard so far. I'd like to see a preliminary plan for the content development project – with approximate costs and estimated time to completion.

Do not simply say "yes" to this proposal! Instead, play "Let's Pretend."

You: I'd be happy to start working on that. Let's pretend for a moment that I when come back with our preliminary plan, you are completely comfortable with my approach, the estimated costs are within your budget, and the completion dates meet your deadlines ... what would happen at that point?

Notice the critical word "I'd" in "I'd be happy to start working on that." That's a very important part of the message.

"I'd" is short for "I *would*," as in "I *would* be happy to start working on that ... once we establish what will happen if I do." You are *not* saying, "I'm happy to start working on that right now, and you can expect it all first thing tomorrow" – or anything similar! You certainly do not want to make a commitment before the prospect starts talking to you about the future. And the best way to get the prospect to talk about the future is to bring it back to the present. *Get the prospect to describe the future to you ... today.*

Here's another example. Suppose you sell security systems and a prospect who is considering an intrusion alarm system for a new warehouse says, "I've received excellent feedback about your company. I'd like to see your approach for the warehouse system, including projected costs and installation time."

To comply with his request, you would have to conduct a site survey, develop an appropriate system to meet all of the requirements, draw a preliminary system schematic, calculate material costs and installation times, package all the information in a proposal, and finally, develop and rehearse your presentation. This is a fairly large commitment on your part … with only the faintest hope that the prospect will actually be persuaded to buy as a result of all your efforts!

Before doing all of that work, use the "Let's Pretend" strategy to determine the likely outcome of your effort. Ask the prospect the following:

You: Let's pretend that I conduct a site survey, develop an appropriate system to meet all of your requirements, draw a preliminary system schematic, calculate material costs and installation times, package all the information and make a presentation where I thoroughly demonstrate how our system would do precisely what you require, which is to deter, detect, and document unauthorized access to the premises. What would happen then?

In fifteen seconds, you've done all the "groundwork" and "made the presentation" – virtually. If the prospect is not willing to make a commitment to an action that is in *your* best interest – and remember, sitting by the phone for days waiting for his decision is definitely not in your best interest – you probably shouldn't commit to doing the work. If you feel you MUST do the work in this situation, charge for it! Agree to apply the initial fee to the project if it is awarded to you. That strategy won't guarantee that you'll get the sale, but at the very least, you'll get paid for your efforts.

THINK TWICE!

Getting the prospect to describe the future today prevents you from being set up. If the prospect can't, or won't, make a commitment that is in your best interest, you must think twice before agreeing to the request to "do the groundwork" or "present your findings."

TEST YOUR UNDERSTANDING

WHY SHOULD YOU PLAY "LET'S PRETEND?"

SEE ANSWER BELOW.

BEHAVIORS

REFLECT ON THE "GROUNDWORK" THAT PROSPECTS TYPICALLY ASK YOU TO DO. FOR THOSE ACTIVITIES THAT GO BEYOND "ROUTINE" — AND YOU MUST BE THE JUDGE OF THAT — DEVELOP A "LET'S PRETEND" QUESTION THAT WILL HELP THE PROSPECT PAINT A PICTURE OF THE FUTURE THAT WOULD RESULT FROM YOUR EFFORTS.

Answer: The "Let's Pretend" strategy gives you an opportunity to measure your prospect's commitment to a future action of mutual benefit, AND measure his willingness and comfort level describing that future commitment. These are indicators of the likelihood of that commitment being honored.

SANDLER
RULE #26

PEOPLE BUY IN SPITE OF THE HARD SELL, NOT BECAUSE OF IT

Have you ever built a proposal or recommendation around your reasons, rather than the prospect's?

- What is the "hard sell?"

- Can it ever *sound* "soft?"

- Whose reasons should be driving the sales discussion?

> SOMETIMES, "CONSULTATIVE" SELLING ISN'T ALL THAT CONSULTATIVE.

You might think that the "hard sell" approach is a thing of the past in professional sales. That's because most sales organizations have adopted some form of "consultative" selling model, where the salesperson aims to "partner" with the prospect in an effort to develop an appropriate solution.

In theory, that approach makes sense. In practice, however, even though there's a lot of talk about "partnering" and being "consultative," too many salespeople still rely on, and structure their selling approach and eventual presentation around, things like:

- The features, benefits, and unique selling points of the product or service

- Their company's history
- The product's reputation for reliability
- Their customer testimonials
- And so on.

Salespeople raise all of these subjects in an effort to *guide* the prospect to a buying decision – even though they don't know what, if anything, is causing pain in the prospect's world.

WHOSE REASONS ARE YOU TALKING ABOUT?

When you build your sales approach around *your reasons* for the prospect to buy, it's still the *hard sell,* even if your demeanor is not aggressive or demanding. When people end up buying from you after you make such appeals, they're buying in spite of your hard sell, not because of it. You need the prospect's reasons!

Make the effort to discover the *prospect's specific reasons* for buying your product or service, as well as their criteria for buying from one company rather than another. Then, structure your approach and presentation around what you have discovered.

SHOULD YOU EVEN BE PURSUING THIS?

If your product or service, or your company, can't meet at least some of the prospect's requirements, rethink whether it makes sense to pursue the opportunity any further. If there is no connection between what you offer and what's going on in this person's world, the "hard sell" – whatever form it may take – is not going to create that connection.

(See also Sandler Rule # 27: *You Can't Sell Anybody Anything – They Must Discover They Want It.*)

TEST YOUR UNDERSTANDING

HOW CAN A MILD-MANNERED SALESPERSON STILL BE GUILTY OF THE "HARD SELL?"

SEE ANSWER BELOW.

Answer: The "hard sell" is not necessarily the result of an aggressive or overbearing presentation – although that would certainly qualify. The "hard sell" is what occurs when we focus a presentation almost exclusively on OUR reasons and justifications for the prospect to buy rather than the prospect's reasons.

BEHAVIORS

Figure out who's reasons are motivating you. Is your natural tendency to tell your prospects why they should buy your product or service? Do you habitually enumerate and drive home the same benefits and advantages you "know" they will enjoy? If so, you're trying to sell with your reasons, not the prospect's.

Make a list of the benefits and advantages that are unique to your product, service and company. In other words, what do you and your company "bring to the table" that a prospect can't possibly obtain from your competitors? Once you have answered this, determine exactly what a prospect would miss out on by NOT doing business with you. (You will utilize this information with the next Rule.)

SANDLER
RULE #27

YOU CAN'T SELL ANYBODY ANYTHING – THEY MUST DISCOVER THEY WANT IT

Have you ever issued a "call to action" that didn't produce any action?

- People don't buy on your say-so.

- Use a better approach.

- Ask, "What would that mean to you?"

> HOW DO YOU FEEL WHEN SOMEONE TELLS YOU TO EAT YOUR VEGETABLES?

Do you remember, years ago, when your mother told you to eat your vegetables? The more she pressed you to eat them, the more you resisted – even when she explained the benefits of eating vegetables (such as helping you to grow up big and strong) and even when she pointed out good moral reasons for doing so (such as your obligation to remember the many people in the world who didn't have fresh vegetables to eat). She pressed, you resisted. It became a predictable routine.

At some psychological level, due in part to those kinds of early childhood experiences, people generally don't like to be told what to do or how to act.

RESISTANCE IS PRE-PROGRAMMED!

As a rule, prospects are programmed to resist salespeople who try, directly or indirectly, to tell them what to do. Regardless of how "right" you may be about what could benefit the prospect, regardless of how many features and functions you can cite, regardless of how convincingly and enthusiastically you explain the benefits and advantages of your product or service, regardless of all this, prospects will have a tendency to resist when you tell them to "eat their vegetables." They simply aren't going to buy on your say-so.

Rather than "selling by telling," a better strategy is to ask questions or relate third-party stories that allow a prospect to discover the benefits and advantages of your product or service. When you ask a question that leads to a discovery, the prospect "owns" the discovery. (See Sandler Rule #15, *The Best Presentation You Will Ever Make, the Prospect Will Never See.*) People may push back, directly or indirectly, if you tell them to "eat their vegetables," but if you let them reach their own conclusions, they typically won't argue with their own data. Instead, they'll ask you to pass the spinach!

"MANY OF OUR CUSTOMERS FOUND ..."

Here's an example of a question that could help the prospect discover that he wants something:

> *You:* Many or our customers found that by installing our real-time tolerance adjustment procedures, they were able to increase widget production by an average of 12 percent. What benefit, if any, would there be for your company from a 12 percent increase in your widget production?

If the *prospect* identifies benefits, follow up with questions that expand the discovery:

You: What would that mean for the company?

You: What would that allow the company to do?

You: What would that mean for you?

Each answer – each additional discovery – helps build a case for buying your product or service. Now the case for "eating the vegetables" is being built by the prospect … not you!

```
┌─────────────────────────────────────────┐
│                                           │
│            TEST YOUR                      │
│         UNDERSTANDING                     │
│                                           │
│                                           │
│       WHY WOULD A PROSPECT                │
│       RESIST OR REJECT YOUR               │
│        PRODUCT OR SERVICE                 │
│       - AFTER YOU'VE CLEARLY              │
│          TOLD HIM ALL THE                 │
│      REASONS HE SHOULD BUY?               │
│                                           │
└─────────────────────────────────────────┘
```

SEE ANSWER BELOW.

BEHAVIORS

USING THE UNIQUE BENEFITS OF YOUR PRODUCT OR SERVICE AND COMPANY THAT YOU IDENTIFIED DURING THE BEHAVIORS FOR RULE #26, DEVELOP QUESTIONS YOU CAN ASK TO HELP YOUR PROSPECTS DISCOVER THE VALUE OF THOSE BENEFITS FOR THEMSELVES.

Answer: In general, people don't like to be TOLD what to do or how to act. This tendency is likely the result of early childhood experiences and programming. Let's say you're the prospect. You may have been TOLD what to do by adults who provided some strange justification for their instructions that you either didn't understand or that didn't fit your world. When you run into a salesperson who tries to do the same thing, you may push back.

SANDLER
RULE #28

WHEN UNDER ATTACK – FALL BACK

Have you ever found yourself in conflict with a prospect or customer?

- Who's OK?

- Who's not?

- Keep the prospect or customer from digging in.

There is a popular saying: "A good offense is the best defense." While

> IS THE BEST DEFENSE REALLY A GOOD OFFENSE?

this may hold true in some arenas, in selling situations it usually doesn't make for very good strategy.

The other myth that connects to this rule sounds like this: "The customer is always right." The prospect or customer is not "always right," but he definitely *is* the judge and jury.

So: How do you respond when you are under attack – being reprimanded for something, rightly or wrongly, for instance? If you take a so-called "good offense" approach by attempting to explain, justify, or defend your position, or by pointing out flaws in your "opponent's" reasoning, you will likely cause your accuser to dig his heels in. Your "good offense" will only make the prospect or customer feel "not OK."

Assuming the customer is "always right," on the other hand, can also delivers some interesting outcomes – like your making promises that you can't possibly keep.

In sales, the better option is simply to *fall back*.

WHAT "FALLING BACK" SOUNDS LIKE

Suppose your company missed a promised delivery date and the customer called to let you know how upset he is. Rather than try to explain about the trucking company's delay, which was out of your control, you could fall back. Here is what that might sound like:

You: Bill, I know that you must be upset about the order arriving a day late. I'm sure it wouldn't do any good to explain what happened. I imagine that you have made up your mind never to do business with our company again. Would that be a fair statement?

It's hard to fight with someone who surrenders up front. In this case, the customer would likely reaffirm his displeasure about the late delivery, but would just as likely back away from the idea of *never* doing business with your company. If the customer had decided never to do business with you again, why would he be investing time in this conversation?

The customer will probably ask for an explanation. After explaining the situation and the measures you have taken to ensure it doesn't happen again, you could proceed with something like this:

You: Bill, if you were in my shoes, what would you do to make things right?

NEGOTIATION BY FALLING BACK

Or consider a different situation: A customer asks for a concession you can't make. When you come under this kind of pressure, you could attempt to explain your position and justify your on-the-spot denial of the customer's request. But what would that lead to? A session of verbal arm-wrestling that ends with the customer saying some variation of, "After all the business I've given you …!"

Instead, you could fall back and gently channel the customer's emotional energy away from hostility and toward creativity.

Customer: That's what we want from you: A box of ripitz for every case of widgets. And that's what we're going to get.

You: Tom, I get the feeling that unless we can provide you with a free box of ripitz with every case of widgets, we've lost your business.

Customer: You're darn close to losing it.

You: And even if I could come up with an alternative to a box of ripitz, it wouldn't make any difference, would it?

Customer: It might.

You: Well, if you were in my shoes, understanding the constraints I'm under, what alternatives would you come up with?

"Falling back" takes the wind out of the customer's sails and makes it possible for you to have a conversation in which each side is OK. Once the emotional intensity is reduced, and nobody is under attack, you have a better chance of working toward a solution.

TEST YOUR UNDERSTANDING

WHAT IS THE PRIMARY BENEFIT OF "FALLING BACK?"

SEE ANSWER BELOW.

BEHAVIORS

IDENTIFY TWO SITUATIONS WHERE YOU WERE "UNDER ATTACK" FROM A PROSPECT OR CUSTOMER. FOR EACH INSTANCE, DETERMINE WHAT YOU COULD HAVE SAID OR DONE TO "FALL BACK" AND EASE THE SITUATION.

Answer: "Falling back" removes the emotional element of the interaction. A prospect is less likely to fight with a salesperson who surrenders up front. Once the emotional element is removed, both parties can have an "intellectual" – and more productive – conversation.

SANDLER
RULE #29

YOUR METER'S
ALWAYS RUNNING

Have you ever blurred the line between "friend" and "customer?"

- Professional standards and priorities matter.

- Is this your customer – or your buddy?

- Don't blur the lines.

> "HEY, COULD YOU DO ME ONE LITTLE FAVOR?"

We already know that our demeanor and our communication style create an image with prospects. In our prospect's mind, that image is a reflection of our company. We don't treat a brand new prospect the same way we would treat a member of the Saturday night bowling team we've been sharing beers and bad jokes with for five years.

The value of having a professional demeanor with *new* contacts is obvious. But what about clients with whom you have developed a long-term relationship? What about the people with whom you *have* developed a friendship? Is it all right to let your guard down with them?

DOING BUSINESS WITH FRIENDS

Becoming friends with a customer may change the dynamics of the relationship, but it doesn't change the nature of the relationship. You and your customer may be more comfortable communicating with one another. That's good. Regardless of how comfortable you two become, however, you still have a "buyer-seller" relationship to maintain. And if you are a professional, that relationship will take precedence over the friendship.

Why? Because becoming chummy with your customer blurs the relationship. Becoming chummy opens the door for "little favors" – price or delivery concessions, for example, that become, in the customer's mind, nothing more than a friendly request. The "favor," if granted, holds little significance, even if the salesperson had to go out of his way to grant it. After all, isn't that what friends are for? To look out for each other?

Similarly, the salesperson may feel that it's OK to make a change to the customer's order – and justify the decision with an explanation like this: "It was only a minor change – I didn't think you'd mind."

In each case, both the friendship and the business relationship will be compromised.

THE METER IS ON!

You can be a friend to your clients and customers – lending a sympathetic ear when necessary (but never seeking one), offering advice when appropriate – as long as the friendship doesn't overshadow the business relationship. A professional cab driver doesn't turn off the meter, no matter how good the conversation is with the passenger; similarly a professional salesperson doesn't do personal favors that conflict with his professional priorities.

You are a salesperson *first*. Keep it that way – or give someone else in your organization the responsibility for handling the account! Be careful: Once the relationship becomes "blurred," it's almost impossible to refocus it.

TEST YOUR UNDERSTANDING

WHAT ARE THE BENEFITS OF DEVELOPING A FRIENDSHIP WITH A CUSTOMER? WHAT ARE THE DANGERS?

SEE ANSWER BELOW.

BEHAVIORS

EXAMINE YOUR RELATIONSHIP WITH EACH OF YOUR CLIENTS AND CUSTOMERS AND IDENTIFY ANY THAT MAY HAVE BECOME (OR ARE ON THE VERGE OF BECOMING) A BIT TOO "CHUMMY." IT MAY BE DIFFICULT TO "PUT THE GENIE BACK IN THE BOTTLE," BUT YOU CAN AT LEAST COMMIT TO NOT LETTING THE PROFESSIONAL RELATIONSHIP WEAKEN ANY FURTHER.

Answer: The benefit is that the friendship is likely to make it easier to communicate. The danger is that the friendship may blur the boundaries of the professional relationship and devalue what each party brings to it.

SANDLER
RULE #30

YOU CAN'T LOSE ANYTHING YOU DON'T HAVE

Have you ever wasted time and effort on a sale that you weren't going to close anyway?

- What are you afraid of?

- Do you suffer from the scarcity mindset?

- Are you an amateur or a professional?

The fear of losing a sale that has yet to be completed haunts too many salespeople.

This fear prevents us from asking the questions that need to be asked. This fear prevents us from doing what needs to be done to either a) close the sale ... or b) discover that the opportunity didn't really measure up after all, and then move on.

> ARE YOU AFRAID OF "ALIENATING" SOMEONE WHO ISN'T BUYING ANYTHING FROM YOU?

WHAT IS GOING ON?

When the selling process starts to drag on, when a prospect doesn't follow through with a commitment or otherwise stalls the process, we need to be assertive – which is different from "aggressive" – and address the issues directly with the prospect.

What is going on? What will happen next? As a professional, you have a right and an obligation to ask these questions. Often, however, the fear of "alienating" the prospect and "destroying the opportunity" to close the sale prevents us from taking this kind of action.

If we let this fear stop us from finding out what is actually taking place, and adjusting our plans accordingly, we are amateur, and not professional, salespeople.

REALITY CHECK

You can't lose a sale you haven't completed. The only thing you risk by addressing the prospect's delaying tactics directly is the "risk" of uncovering the truth. And, if the truth is that you're not going to close the sale, why on earth would you want to postpone learning about that?

Psychologists say that one cause of the thinking that keeps salespeople from facing reality with such prospects is a "scarcity" mentality. People with a scarcity mentality believe that there is not enough to go around. They believe that real opportunities are lacking. They believe that they must seize every opportunity, because if they don't, someone else will seize it. Can you see how such thinking would cause you to hang on to dubious opportunities longer than appropriate and avoid behavior that might reveal the true value of the opportunity?

"I believe this sale will eventually come through.

"Therefore, I choose not to antagonize the prospect whom I believe to be acting on my behalf, even though I have had no proof that this prospect is acting on my behalf.

"If I were to antagonize this person, he might disapprove of me, and might turn to someone else."

Where does such thinking come from? Typically, from early childhood programming – the messages you received from your parents and other authority figures from the time you began to walk until mom and dad sent you off to school. You may have been told to count your blessings. Not bad advice, unless it was followed by the admonition to do so, *because blessings are few and far between.* Were you told that *a penny saved was a penny earned?* Were you told that *money doesn't grow on trees?* What was the emotional message behind those teachings? The word "hoarding" comes to mind. Isn't that what you are doing when you won't let go of a prospect who doesn't measure up?

Were you told that life is a contest or a *struggle?* The implication behind that message is that you are either a winner or a loser. If your actions are guided by that type of thinking, then the act of letting go of an opportunity, even a poor quality opportunity, means that you will lose and someone else, perhaps your competitor, will win.

"I HATE PROSPECTING"

Another element that drives salespeople's fears and causes them to hang on to poor quality opportunities longer than they should is the realization that they will have to replace the prospect. Some salespeople will go to almost any length to avoid prospecting. For many, the *perceived* pain of prospecting is greater than the *actual* pain of income that is lost while they are hanging on to an opportunity that has stalled.

If you've been in the stalled sale situation, then you know that eventually, the balance tips in the other direction and the *real* pain of prospecting is far less than the pain of continuing to pursue an opportunity that is going nowhere. You may remember the old commercial for Fram oil filters, with the world-weary mechanic who advised motorists who went too long between oil changes that they could "pay me now … or pay me later." The principle is precisely the same here. You can pay the small price now – prospecting – to replace the poor quality prospect. Or, you can pay the big price later – wasted time and energy, frustration, disappointment, and of course, no sale – and *still* be left with the need to prospect.

(See also Rule #7, *You Never Have to Like Prospecting, You Just Have to Do It,* and Rule #31: *Close the Sale or Close the File.*)

TEST YOUR UNDERSTANDING

WHAT IS THE UNDERLYING REASON FOR HANGING ON TO OPPORTUNITIES THAT HAVE STALLED, RATHER THAN TAKING ACTION TO REPLACE THEM IN YOUR PIPELINE?

SEE ANSWER BELOW.

BEHAVIORS

IDENTIFY ANY OPPORTUNITIES THAT YOU ARE CURRENTLY HANGING ON TO OUT OF FEAR. COMMIT TO HAVING A CONVERSATION WITH THOSE PROSPECTS AND EITHER OBTAIN A FIRM COMMITMENT FROM THEM TO MOVE THE PROCESS FORWARD IN A TIMELY MANNER — OR CLOSE THE FILE.

Answer: The underlying reason is usually fear. Fear that another opportunity won't come along; fear that if you let go of the opportunity, somebody else will claim it; fear that you will have to go out and proactively prospect in order to find another opportunity.

SANDLER
RULE #31

CLOSE THE SALE
OR CLOSE THE FILE

Have you ever missed a signal that there was really "no deal?"

- Is this really the best fit?

- Is this person willing to work with you?

- Could your efforts be more productive somewhere else?

Many salespeople are taught to "never take 'no' for an answer." When the prospect says "no," the salesperson mentally consults his "overcoming stalls and objections" list, and fires back a response designed to turn the "no" into a "yes." Of course, the prospect has his list

> KNOW WHEN
> TO MOVE ON.

of responses, too. The process continues ad infinitum until someone, or someone's list, is exhausted.

YOU MUST KNOW WHERE YOU ARE

There comes a point when you must either close the sale or close the file. The odds are good that you already know, intuitively, when you reach that point with a prospect. If you don't know, or think you don't, ask a sales manager or colleague for some perspective on the matter.

Continually pushing for the "yes," continually ignoring the possibility that your product or service may not be the best fit, continually refusing to take a "no" that's stated directly or indirectly, will lead you down a dead-end path. The result will be wasted time, effort, and resources that could have been invested in other opportunities. If the prospect's buying decision is going to be "no," common sense dictates that you elicit that decision as quickly as possible. It bears repeating: The sooner you find out that you are not going to make a sale, the sooner you can direct your energy to more profitable pursuits!

If you are thoroughly knowledgeable about your product or service and understand the situations it was designed to address, the problems it was designed to solve, and the results it was designed to achieve, you'll be able to diagnose a prospect's situation and determine whether your product or service really is a good fit. If it is not, the process stops. If it is, but the prospect will not help you to develop a mutually committed business relationship, the process stops in that case, too.

WHAT IS A "GOOD FIT?"

A "good fit" is *only* a good fit if you can deliver it for the investment the prospect is willing and able to make, and in the manner and timeframe the prospect requires. If you can't meet all of the requirements that define a good fit for this person, recognize that continuing to pursue the opportunity will only lead to an eventual "no." Acknowledge the eventual "no" right now ... and move on.

You can hide from it, do your best to avoid it, even refuse to recognize it, but a "no" today is still a "no" tomorrow. Close the sale – or close the file!

(See also Rule #43, *You Don't Learn How to Win by Getting a "Yes" – You Learn How to Win by Getting a "No."*)

TEST YOUR UNDERSTANDING

HOW WILL AN UNDERSTANDING OF THE "GOOD FIT" CONCEPT MAKE IT EASIER FOR YOU TO CLOSE THE FILE ON SALES THAT ARE NOT MOVING FORWARD?

SEE ANSWER BELOW.

BEHAVIORS

EXAMINE ANY OPPORTUNITIES THAT HAVE BEEN DRAGGING ON FOR A WHILE. TAKE A HARD LOOK AT THE OPPORTUNITY AND DETERMINE WHETHER YOUR PRODUCT OR SERVICE IS TRULY THE VERY BEST FIT FOR THE SITUATION. IF IT'S NOT, CLOSE THE FILE. IF IT IS, ADDRESS THE ISSUE WITH THE PROSPECT AND DETERMINE EXACTLY WHAT IT WILL TAKE TO GET THE PROCESS MOVING. IF THE PROSPECT IS UNWILLING TO MAKE AN ACCEPTABLE COMMITMENT, CLOSE THE FILE.

Answer: If the selling process has stalled and a critical analysis reveals that your product or service doesn't satisfy all of your prospect's needs in a better manner than your competitors, then it's time to let go. Prospects ultimately gravitate to products and services that provide the very best fit for their situation. If that's not you, close the file and move on.

SANDLER
RULE #32

GET AN I.O.U. FOR EVERYTHING YOU DO

*Do you ever go above and beyond the call
– and get little or no credit for it?*

• Are you giving "free" service routinely?

• Customers should notice the effort.

• Use I.O.U.s to set up a future win.

> THE CUSTOMER SHOULD NOTICE AND REMEMBER THE EFFORT YOU ARE PUTTING FORTH ON HIS BEHALF.

It's always surprising to learn during our seminars how many salespeople are willing to perform "free" services for their customers.

Apparently, the salesperson believes that, by performing free services, the customer will give him some consideration in return. That's not a bad idea if the customer knows how to "mind-read," (See Rule #13, *No Mind Reading*), but most of the time, it doesn't lead to much in the way of revenue.

YOU ALREADY DO TOO MUCH "FREE" WORK

Selling is one of the few professions where much of the preliminary work we do is, technically, "free." Do we charge a prospect money for the time, effort, and energy that goes into creating a proposal? Can you see yourself going to the nearest multiplex cinema, walking up to the ticket counter and telling the attendant, "I'm going inside to see the movie. If I like it, I'll pay you on the way out?" Can you imagine telling a cab driver that you'll let him know when you like the ride enough for him to turn the meter on? But this is essentially what happens every day when we interact with prospects who are "considering" doing business with us.

Once prospects turn into customers, we need to be quite clear about what we are putting into the relationship. Of course, no one is suggesting that you should *stop* performing services for your customers. This Rule is saying something very different: Look for ways you can help the customer to *see and notice* the effort you are putting forth on his behalf.

Believe it or not, some customers believe that your company pays you to perform these "no-charge" services! That's not the case, of course, and your customer should know that.

THE ART OF GETTING AN I.O.U.

Here's a simple scenario that illustrates the point.

Customer: Hal, can you bring a few extra cases of #243 by the office Saturday morning? We're out.
You: Fred, I'd like to help, but there may be a problem. Let me ask you this, how badly do you need them?

(Your intention, of course, is to take the cases to him.)

Customer: I really need them badly.

You: How long are you going to be in your office this morning?

Customer: I'll be here all morning.

You: Call you back in a few minutes. I need to see if I can reschedule a few things I had lined up for Saturday morning.

You: (When you call back.) Good news – I can get them to you Saturday morning by 10:00 am.

Your first move could have been, "No problem. I'll be glad to bring them over Saturday morning." As played out above, however, the customer received a subtle message that you were going "above and beyond the call of duty" by changing previous plans.

After several situations like the one above, when you are "apples to apples" with the competition, your I.O.U.s alone could get you the next order. You don't have to *remind* the customer of what you've done – the I.O.U.s are there!

```
┌─────────────────────────────────────────┐
│                                           │
│            TEST YOUR                       │
│         UNDERSTANDING                      │
│                                           │
│                                           │
│         WHY COLLECT AN I.O.U.             │
│         FROM A GOOD CLIENT                │
│        FOR A SERVICE OR FAVOR             │
│           YOU'D GLADLY DO?                │
│                                           │
└─────────────────────────────────────────┘
```

SEE ANSWER BELOW.

BEHAVIORS

IDENTIFY THE ADDED VALUE SERVICES YOU SOMETIMES PERFORM FOR CUSTOMERS. DEVELOP A FEW STRATEGIES FOR COLLECTING AN I.O.U. FOR THEM.

Answer: Collecting an I.O.U. positions the service as "added value" to the product or service you provide. Not collecting an I.O.U. can leave the client with the impression that the extra services are part and parcel of the original purchase and therefore represent no added value. With that impression, customers can quickly develop the habit of asking — and expecting — such favors on a regular basis.

SANDLER
RULE #33

ON YOUR WAY TO THE BANK, KEEP ONE EYE OVER YOUR SHOULDER

Have you ever lost a sale you thought was closed?

- Is it really "closed?"

- What could go wrong?

- What future problems can you solve right now?

> **WHAT DO YOU HAVE TO DO TO MAKE THE COMMISSION BANKABLE?**

You completed your presentation; the prospect said "yes," and committed to have the purchase order faxed to you in the morning. It took longer than you planned and you jumped through more hoops than you care to admit, but it was worth it: the sale represents a sizable share of your quota, a profitable piece of business for the company, and a nice commission check for you. It's time to shake hands, head for your office, and wait for that fax to come in.

Or is it?

HOW CLOSED IS "CLOSED?"

Before that commission is *bankable,* the sale must be closed ... really closed. That means the purchase order must be received, the order processed, and the product or service delivered and accepted by the prospect. Before you leave your prospect's office, ask yourself: What internal problems could disrupt the process now?

We're not talking about buyer's remorse here. The questions to consider under this rule sound like this: Is there another decision maker, or perhaps a committee, who could veto the decision? Does an incumbent supplier have a "last look" opportunity to better your offer? Could the intended purchase be put on hold for any reason – including, say, an obligation to "run the decision past" a higher-up you have not met?

If your answer to any of these questions is "I'm not sure," you're in trouble.

DO YOU KNOW FOR SURE THAT YOU'RE GOING TO THE BANK?

Identify all the potential internal roadblocks that could prevent the sale from closing. Ideally, these issues should be addressed and resolved prior to giving the presentation. If any remain unsettled, address them *immediately* after obtaining the prospect's decision. If there is even the slightest possibility of a roadblock, look for a way to discuss the issue directly, and find a way to remove the potential barrier. If the "closed" sale isn't really closed, it's better to find out now about organizational issues that could keep you from going to the bank.

(See also Rule #6: *Don't Buy Back Tomorrow the Product or Service You Sold Today,* which deals with buyer's remorse, and Rule #20, *The Bottom Line of Professional Selling Is Going to the Bank.*)

TEST YOUR UNDERSTANDING

You've closed the deal, obtained the signed purchase order, and shaken hands with your customer. What still remains to be done?

SEE ANSWER BELOW.

BEHAVIORS

Look back on past situations where a "done deal" came undone... and identify the circumstances that caused the derailment. Figure out what you could have done to recognize the situation earlier, and what you could have done to prevent it.

Answer: Until the product or service is delivered and accepted by the customer, the deal can unravel – despite the signed order and despite the handshake. You must anticipate anything that can still go wrong within the buying organization ... and be prepared to deal with it before it derails your sale.

PART THREE:

COURSE-CORRECT

Remind yourself of what's easy to forget.

SANDLER
RULE #34

WORK SMART, NOT HARD

Have you ever stayed with a stalled prospect for too long?

- What's the difference between "smart work" and "hard work"?
- The "all-or-nothing" mentality.
- Are you trying to make a point?

Ronald Reagan once said, "It's true that hard work never killed anyone — but I figure, why take the chance?"

There seems to be a belief that the harder you work, the more you are likely to accomplish. Certainly, persistence and hard work do pay off in some endeavors: World class athletes, for instance, don't become "world class" overnight. Persistence and hard work is integral to their plan. But, their training regimen is smart. They know their limits, they focus their efforts, and they pace themselves. They don't overexert or take shortcuts in an effort to speed up the process.

> TIE DOWN THE SALE WITH A MONKEY'S PAW.

ARE YOU WORKING SMART?

Working *smart* in the sales arena means using an *efficient* system to identify, qualify, and develop selling opportunities. The system should revolve around *specific criteria* that must be met at various stages in order to keep the process moving toward a completed sale. If the criteria can't be met, it's time to abandon the opportunity and pursue another one that is more viable.

Continuing to pursue an opportunity that has stalled – perhaps because you've already invested so much time in it, or because you're out to prove something to someone – is not a productive use of your time. That's working hard. But it definitely isn't working smart. (See also Rule #30: *You Can't Lose Anything You Don't Have.*)

Consider the case of the salesperson who is fixated on the "big deal." Sometimes that stubborn approach leads to a lot of *hard* work over a period of months (or years!) and a "no" answer … when a little *smart* work could lead to a "yes" answer in the short term that gets your foot in the door.

IT DOESN'T HAVE TO BE ALL OR NOTHING

If you ever watched a cruise ship come into dock you might have noticed the huge heavy ropes that tie the ship to the dock. How do they get those ropes from the bow of the ship – about ten stories high – to the pier? They use what's called a Monkey's Paw – a small ball tied to a small diameter line, tied to the big rope. A member of the ship's crew throws the ball to the dockhand on the pier, and the dockhand pulls the ball, the small line, and the heavy rope to the dock!

What has that got to do with sales? Well, if you sell a big-ticket item, it might be difficult for your prospect to make an all-or-nothing decision in favor of a new supplier. But what if you were to break up the sale into smaller pieces?

For instance: could you sell a research project, or a study? Is there a one-day consulting project you could do? Is there a thirty-day trial you could sell? Ask yourself what you could sell that is smaller in scope, cost, or perceived risk. Your prospect may not be ready to commit to the large sale, but may be ready to make an initial smaller commitment. The strategy takes your client "off the street" and lowers the buyer-seller wall.

So throw out a Monkey's Paw. Get a little piece of the action and then help yourself to more of it, a little at a time.

DON'T SET TRAPS FOR YOURSELF!

There are many ways that salespeople cheat themselves out of income by *working hard* – when they could be *working smart*. Often, the hard work they perform is the result of some kind of trap they've set for themselves.

Is your *hard work* connected to making some kind of abstract point about (for instance) whether or not the world is "fair?" Is your *hard work* connected to earning approval from someone? (A prospect? Your boss? Your family members?) Watch out for these traps! The most effective professional salespeople learn to step around them.

TEST YOUR UNDERSTANDING

WHAT DOES "WORKING SMART" REQUIRE?

SEE ANSWER BELOW.

BEHAVIORS

TAKE A CLOSE, HONEST LOOK AT THE MOTIVES AND MOTIVATIONS THAT DRIVE YOUR APPROACH TO SELLING. ARE YOUR ACTIONS GUIDED BY A SYSTEM WITH SPECIFIC BENCHMARKS THAT YOU MUST HIT TO KEEP THE PROCESS MOVING? OR DO YOU SOMETIMES FIND YOURSELF PURSUING OR CHASING OPPORTUNITIES FOR EMOTIONAL REASONS?

COMMIT TO TAKING ACTIONS THAT ARE GUIDED BY MEASURABLE CRITERIA, NOT BY EMOTIONAL REASONS THAT MAY CAUSE YOU TO PURSUE SOME CLEARLY INAPPROPRIATE OPPORTUNITIES OR HANG ON TOO LONG TO OTHERS WHEN THEY NO LONGER MEET YOUR CRITERIA.

Answer: Working smart requires the use of a systematic approach for developing selling opportunities. Your system must define exactly what must happen at each stage of the process in order to keep your sale moving forward.

SANDLER
RULE #35

IF YOUR COMPETITION DOES IT, STOP DOING IT RIGHT AWAY

Have you ever lost a deal because you didn't effectively distinguish yourself from the competition?

- Where is the edge?

- Amateurs rely too heavily on product or service.

- Can you stand on your own?

Years ago, there was a Xerox commercial that showed salesman after salesman presenting himself to a prospect and saying, "And it's just like a Xerox!" In the final seconds of the commercial, a particularly poised and confident salesman says, "Ahem – it is a Xerox!"

> COME UP WITH A GAME PLAN THAT IS UNIQUE.

Some ad agency must have made a fortune on that commercial. Interestingly, the copiers all looked pretty much alike. So did the salespeople! Maybe the ad agency could have improved the message a little bit by both making the "superior" product and the "superior" salesperson stand out somehow.

Where was the edge? In the product? In the salesperson?

You are a professional salesperson. No doubt you represent a good product or service. You and what you sell are not, however, one and the same.

Amateur salespeople rely too heavily on their product or service. The professional can stand on his own. You should be unique in the approach you take to presenting not only your product, but also yourself.

DO YOU KNOW WHAT THE COMPETITION IS DOING?

Take a look at your competition and see whether you can come up with a game plan that is unique. For example, if your competition is relying on a 70-slide PowerPoint presentation to run the meeting, what can you do differently?

FIND A WAY TO STAND ON YOUR OWN

There is *something* you can do to stand on your own, *something* you can do that will be unique in your corner of the marketplace. If you are truly a professional, you will find out what that "something" is – and build it into what you do, day in and day out.

One classic opportunity for differentiation lies in targeting particular "added-value" features and benefits your company offers to accommodate the unique needs of specific prospects and customers, thereby creating a truly one-of-a-kind connection that no competitor can match. This is an art, not a science. In today's technology-driven, feature-rich selling environment, however, it is definitely an art worth mastering.

If you choose to go down this road, remember that "added-value" is only valuable *if the prospect discovers a need for what you are offering*. Without this acknowledgement, the "added-value" becomes added "expense" in the prospect's eyes and a reason to negotiate price or reject the product altogether. You must make the shift in your own mind, and in the mind of your prospect, from vendor to advisor. You must, in short, diagnose before you prescribe … and you must then connect the dots in a way that your competitors can't.

TEST YOUR UNDERSTANDING

DOES THE WAY THE COMPETITION IS SELLING MATTER? IF SO WHY?

SEE ANSWER BELOW.

BEHAVIORS

MAKE A LIST OF TEN THINGS YOU OR YOUR ORGANIZATION CAN OFFER THAT THE COMPETITION CANNOT. PRIORITIZE THE LIST ACCORDING TO WHAT YOU KNOW A CURRENT PROSPECT OF YOURS WOULD CONSIDER MOST IMPORTANT.

Answer: Yes. You must know what the competition is doing, ... so you can establish a unique position for yourself and your organization.

SANDLER
RULE #36

ONLY DECISION MAKERS CAN GET OTHERS TO MAKE DECISIONS

Have you ever lost a deal because <u>you</u> didn't make the right decisions?

- Control your process.
- Make good "go/no-go" decisions.
- Act in a way that supports your decisions.

Selling is a development process that is driven by the decisions of you, the seller.

> YOU, THE SALESPERSON, HAVE MANY DECISIONS TO MAKE.

Selling is what takes place when you lead the prospect through a step by step process, each step of which may lead to the prospect's disqualification and removal from the process. If you do not disqualify the prospect opportunity, the sale moves forward, and eventually culminates in the prospect making a buying decision.

While the prospect has one basic decision to make during this process – to buy or not to buy – you, the salesperson, have many decisions to make. At each step in the process, you must make a "go/no-go" decision. That is, you must decide if your prospect is qualified to move to the next step and whether or not to continue to invest your time and your company's resources in the process. These are critical decisions. You must make them in a timely manner.

Your ability to a) make these decisions and b) act in a way that supports your decisions, will determine the length of your selling cycle, and ultimately, the number of sales you close in a given period of time. For you, the professional salesperson, there can be no long period of "thinking it over." The prospect either meets the criteria you've established or he doesn't. You either move the person to the next phase of your selling process or you don't. You are the most important decision maker in the process.

DON'T DRAG YOUR FEET

The more quickly you make your decisions, the shorter your selling cycle and the greater your chances for closing more sales. Dragging your feet on the decision leads to the opposite results – longer selling cycles and fewer sales.

If the development process progresses far enough, you'll be making a presentation for the purpose of obtaining a buying decision. If you have been decisive in making your "go/no-go" decisions along the way, you will be comfortable asking your prospect to commit to making a "buy/don't-buy" decision when he views your presentation. The request will be consistent with the behavior and actions you have exhibited – and modeled for the prospect – all along.

Not only will you be comfortable asking your prospect to make a "yes/no" decision, but because you understand the downside of "think-it-over," you'll be comfortable giving your prospect permission to say "no" – rather than some form of "think it over" – if he has any doubts about your product or service being a best fit for his needs. (See also Rule # 4: *A Decision Not to Make a Decision Is a Decision.*)

TEST YOUR UNDERSTANDING

WHY ARE THE DECISIONS YOU MAKE DURING THE DEVELOPMENT PROCESS MORE IMPORTANT THAN THE PROSPECT'S ULTIMATE BUYING DECISION?

SEE ANSWER BELOW.

Answer: At critical stages during the selling process, you must make decisions to either continue or end the process. Your ability to accurately judge each will determine how many opportunities reach the stage where prospects make buying decisions.

BEHAVIORS

EXAMINE YOUR SELLING PROCESS AND IDENTIFY YOUR SPECIFIC "GO/NO-GO" DECISION POINTS. HOW COMFORTABLE ARE YOU MAKING THOSE DECISIONS?

REFLECT ON YOUR SELLING PRESENTATIONS. HOW COMFORTABLE AND EFFECTIVE ARE YOU GETTING PROSPECTS TO COMMIT TO MAKING A "BUY/DON'T-BUY" DECISION WHEN YOU SCHEDULE THOSE PRESENTATIONS? HOW EFFECTIVE ARE YOU AT ACTUALLY OBTAINING THOSE DECISIONS RATHER THAN ACCEPTING SOME FORM OF "THINK-IT-OVER?"

WHAT IS YOUR RATIO OF TOTAL SCHEDULED PRESENTATIONS TO SCHEDULED PRESENTATIONS WHICH INCLUDE THE PROSPECT'S FIRM COMMITMENT TO MAKE A DECISION? WHAT IS YOUR RATIO OF BUYING DECISIONS OBTAINED FROM PROSPECTS TO THINK-IT-OVERS ACCEPTED FROM PROSPECTS AT THE CONCLUSION OF PRESENTATIONS?

WHAT CONCLUSIONS CAN YOU DRAW FROM THESE BEHAVIORS?

SANDLER
RULE #37

ALL PROSPECTS LIE,
ALL THE TIME

Have you ever wondered why a prospect led you down the wrong path?

- It's true – they do!

- The variable is *why* ... and *about* what.

Okay, it may be a bit of an overstatement to say that *all* prospects lie *all* the time. But the underlying idea is sound, and worth considering closely.

Let's just say that prospects tend to be less than completely truthful *much* of the time. For example, one prospect proclaims

> DON'T BE MISLED.

that he is the decision maker, but doesn't reveal that he has to get an approving nod from the CFO. Another prospect says she is eager to move quickly, but doesn't disclose that the timing for the final decision is still three months away.

WHY DO PROSPECTS LIE?

Many prospects feel that it's necessary to mislead salespeople in this manner. Perhaps they believe they are protecting themselves from the sometimes overeager salesperson who is ready to pounce at the first sign of a "buying signal." Or perhaps they are covering up vulnerable areas – not the least of which is probably an unwillingness to admit that there are areas they don't know very much about.

To avoid being misled, you will need to ask a few questions to confirm just about everything your prospect tells you. If the prospect says he is the decision maker, ask who else might play a role in the decision ... or who has the power to veto a decision. For the prospect who is eager to move quickly, ask how soon she needs to make a decision ... and what might happen if it took longer.

The television show *House* offers the example of Dr. Gregory House, a cynical physician with an abiding distrust of patients – a distrust rooted in his firm belief in the willingness of all patients to lie. House knows, from personal experience, that patients are more than willing to mislead the people who are trying to help them, even when their own lives are at stake. "It's a basic truth of the human condition that everybody lies," Dr. House opines in one episode. "The only variable is about what." The parallel between patients and prospects almost makes itself.

No. You shouldn't use House's contempt for his patients as your model for behavior in interacting with prospects – but you probably should use his skepticism. Prospects may not lie all the time, but if you proceed as if they did, and then confirm each and every piece of information you receive, you are likely to come away with a more accurate picture of your selling opportunity.

TEST YOUR UNDERSTANDING

HOW CAN ASSUMING THAT "ALL PROSPECTS LIE" SUPPORT A PRODUCTIVE RELATIONSHIP WITH PROSPECTS?

SEE ANSWER BELOW.

BEHAVIORS

IDENTIFY THREE INSTANCES WHERE DOUBLE-CHECKING THE FACTS, SUCH AS A PROSPECT'S PROCLAMATION, "I MAKE ALL THE DECISIONS" OR "MONEY'S NO OBJECT," WOULD HAVE BEEN USEFUL TO YOU.

Answer: This strategy requires you to double-check what prospects tell you (or what you believe they told you). Assuming "all prospects lie" will prevent you from acting on false assumptions and misunderstandings.

SANDLER
RULE #38

THE PROBLEM
THE PROSPECT BRINGS
YOU IS NEVER
THE REAL PROBLEM

Have you ever accepted a prospect's "diagnosis" at face value?

- Don't accept a false premise.

- Do be skeptical.

- Is it really the problem, or is it a symptom?

Too many salespeople rely on a false premise as they attempt to "qualify" and develop a selling opportunity.

The false premise they rely on sounds like this: "Prospects understand their own problems well enough not only to recognize what created those problems, but also to identify suitable solutions when they team up with a salesperson who's willing to ask a few 'probing questions.' "

It sounds implausible when you put it into words, doesn't it? Yet this is precisely the assumption under which most salespeople operate.

Have you ever taken a prospect's "diagnosis" of a problem at face value? It's very easy to do. The more complex the problems are, and the more pressing they seem to be, the less likely it is that prospects will have invested the time to look beyond the symptoms to identify the origins of the problems. This is true even if the prospect should happen to know what to look for, which is, as we know, very often not the case.

In psychiatric medical school, the first lesson students learn is this one:

THE PROBLEM THE PATIENT BRINGS YOU IS NEVER THE REAL PROBLEM

In sales training school, the first lesson to be learned should be:

THE PROBLEM THE PROSPECT BRINGS YOU IS NEVER THE REAL PROBLEM

Your prospect has learned over the years to protect vulnerabilities by not revealing the real problems "up front." Showing you the true "pain" could put the prospect in an unwanted, high-risk situation. (See Rule #37, *All Prospects Lie, All the Time.*) This may, from our point of view, seem illogical. Why would the prospect want to waste his time, or ours? To understand the special logic of the prospect, and the inescapable importance of "saving face" in human relationships, consider the following episode between a husband and a wife.

While surfing the Internet one evening, our prospect sees a movie advertisement and says to his wife, "I'm hearing some good things about the latest Matt Damon movie. You probably don't want to go to that film, do you, honey?"

Wife: "Well, I might like to go."
Prospect: "How about this evening?"
Wife: "Oh, no. Not this evening."

To which our prospect who really would like to go to the movie replies,

Prospect: "I don't feel like going tonight, either."

Our prospect is safe. No vulnerabilities have been exposed!

There's a very similar dynamic in play during the early discussions with any salesperson. For instance, in our industry, people may tell us that members of their sales team have problems with their "closing techniques." We have an obligation to ask whether that is really the problem – or whether the unacceptably low closing ratios are simply a symptom of a deeper issue, such as the company's salespeople spending most or all of their "selling" time with people who have no authority to make decisions. In fact, that's a qualifying problem, not a closing problem.

The next time you are tempted to accept a prospect's assessment of a problem – don't. Relying on prospects in this way is a bad idea. When we do this, we may "buy in" to the prospects' perceptions about their problems, which rarely touch on the real causes, and are often (let's face it) delusional. In addition, we may find ourselves accepting the prospect's focus on apparent "solutions" to improperly diagnosed problems – "solutions" that will be, at best, premature and, at worst, entirely inappropriate.

DIAGNOSIS IS THE SALESPERSON'S RESPONSIBILITY

As professional salespeople, we must have comprehensive knowledge not only about the products and services we sell, but also of the current and potential problems and challenges of the prospects on whom we call. We must know how to diagnose prospects' *perceived* problems – by looking beyond the symptoms and identifying the underlying causes, the real problems to be addressed. If we don't bring that knowledge with us on a sales call, it is unlikely that we will find it when we shake hands with the prospect.

TEST YOUR UNDERSTANDING

HOW CAN YOU AVOID
"SPINNING YOUR WHEELS"
DEVELOPING "SOLUTIONS"
FOR "PROBLEMS" THAT
AREN'T THE REAL ISSUE?

SEE ANSWER BELOW.

BEHAVIORS

MAKE A LIST OF THE SYMPTOMS PROSPECTS TYPICALLY MISTAKE FOR THEIR PROBLEM OR CHALLENGE. THEN, FOR EACH SYMPTOM, IDENTIFY THE TRUE UNDERLYING PROBLEM THAT CAN BE ADDRESSED BY YOUR PRODUCT OR SERVICE.

Answer: You must be knowledgeable enough about your product or service to recognize the real underlying problem when prospects relate to you the SYMPTOMS of those problems. The symptom is not the problem!

SANDLER
RULE #39

WHEN ALL ELSE FAILS, BECOME A CONSULTANT

Have you ever reached the "end of the line" with a prospect – and had no idea what to do to move forward?

- Use the "last resort" question.

- "Can I stop being a salesperson?"

GIVE AWAY
CONCEPTS
– SELL THE
IMPLEMENTATION

You have done everything you possibly can, your techniques have been impeccable, but your prospect, for some reason, still won't buy. You have made several "dummy" moves (See Rule #17, *The Professional Does What He Did As a Dummy – On Purpose*), and you're still stuck.

Here is a "last resort" question that will open up some prospects:

You: "Can I stop being a salesperson for a minute and be a consultant?

Most prospects will say "OK." (In the unlikely event that the prospect doesn't say that, you can respond with a final "dummy" question. For instance: "Are we done?")

When the prospect does say "OK" to the idea of your becoming a consultant for a moment, which is the far more likely outcome, you have an opportunity: You must now "hit" the person as hard as you can with a picture of what will happen if they don't buy your product or service.

Here's what you say — as a consultant.

You: "Here's my problem. I believe that what I've shown you makes sense for you. It's obvious to me that you don't agree. So, how do I tell you, without you becoming upset, that you're not only hurting your production numbers, but also hurting your bottom line by continuing to handle your inventory with your current system?"

Isn't this what consultants are paid to do — give objective, hard-hitting advice? If your prospect had bought your product, wouldn't you actually move into a consultant role after it is delivered?

As you proceed along these lines, you should be ready to share the same insights and expertise that a consultant would. The primary question is not how much knowledge you should be ready to "give away," but rather which *concepts* you are willing to share as you make your case. Whenever you step into "consultant mode," your goal should be to give away concepts, and then sell the implementation of those concepts!

For instance, a concept for reducing handling and warehousing costs is to coordinate the inventorying and ordering processes of materials with projected production schedules to achieve just-in-time deliveries. Implementation would be the IT services and software that ties the production, inventory, and ordering systems together. At this stage of your relationship, your goal should not be to work out a plan for implementation. Clearly, the relationship is not there yet.

When you put on your "consultant's hat," build your advice around the concepts that connect to your value. Your goal is to plant the seed — the concept — and provide information to fire the prospect's imagination — which allows the seed to grow. Then, you sell the implementation. The more a prospect understands the concepts on which your product or service is based and understands how those concepts relate to his problems, concerns, challenges, or goals, the more inclined he will be to buy your implementation. Think of your ideas and product concepts as the compelling review that makes the reader want to buy the book, or the exciting movie trailer that drives the viewer to the box office. When you help the prospect view the implementation of your product or service as the solution to his problems or the pathway for the achievement of his goals, you've taken a big step toward following the much-discussed, but often ignored, consultative selling approach.

TEST YOUR UNDERSTANDING

HOW DOES THE KNOWLEDGE YOU "GIVE AWAY" AS A CONSULTANT PAY YOU BACK WHEN YOU TAKE OFF YOUR CONSULTANT'S "HAT?"

SEE ANSWER BELOW.

BEHAVIORS

IDENTIFY SOME SITUATIONS WHEN BECOMING A "CONSULTANT" WOULD BE APPROPRIATE. DESCRIBE THE SITUATIONS — AND WHAT YOUR RECOMMENDATIONS AS A "CONSULTANT" WOULD BE.

Answer: The knowledge you give away as a consultant helps the prospect better understand his situation ... and more easily recognize your product or service as the solution to his problem or pathway to the achievement of his goals.

SANDLER
RULE #40

FAKE IT 'TIL YOU MAKE IT

Have you ever sent the prospect the message that you "needed" the order?

• Master the art of "singing like you don't need the money."

Some sales are lost because the prospect senses that the salesperson "needs" the order. A salesperson can telegraph these messages through nervous reactions, body language, hesitancy, etcetera.

It's OK to *want* the deal. It's just not OK to need it.

> IT'S OK TO WANT THE DEAL. IT'S JUST NOT OK TO NEED IT.

An effective technique to help you keep your cool when you are tempted to act as though you need the deal is to repeat the following phrase in your mind, over and over again:

I AM FINANCIALLY INDEPENDENT AND I DON'T NEED THE BUSINESS.

There's a country tune about singing "like you don't need the money" that captures basically the same point. No one is suggesting blind denial as a sales strategy, of course, but the power of personal optimism captured in that song title is something that the very best salespeople always manage to broadcast. If you really didn't need the money, if you were financially independent, wouldn't you know what to say? Wouldn't your questions come easier?

Prospect: Why should I buy from you?

You: (Nurturing, but not abrasive) Maybe you shouldn't … but let me ask you a question … (and here you continue with your line of questioning.)

Remember, if you were really financially independent, if you didn't need the business, you would neither act arrogantly nor beg for the business. You wouldn't have to!

HARD NUMBERS

Some people dismiss the "fake it 'til you make it" approach (also known as the "act as if" approach) because they consider it either "unrealistic" or rooted in "denial."

If you are tempted to fast-forward over this selling rule on such grounds, you should stop for just a moment and consider the clinical evidence that supports the "fake it 'til you make it" principle. A recent study of law schools by Segerstrom measured the optimism of first-year law students, and correlated the students' later earning power with their ability to assume the best about themselves, their abilities, and their circumstances. The study, which used a five-point optimism scale, concluded that each and every one-point climb in personal optimism coincided with a $33,000 advantage in annual income a decade later!

We believe that the optimism-to-income curve is even steeper among the best professional salespeople, and we have thousands of practitioners following the Sandler Selling System who prove the point daily.

What "needy" messages are you telegraphing right now? How will you correct them? What positive "act as if" messages could you send instead to yourself – and the prospects and customers you come in contact with every day?

TEST YOUR UNDERSTANDING

"FAKING IT" REFERS TO:

☐ A) YOUR KNOWLEDGE AND EXPERTISE

☐ B) YOUR CONFIDENCE ABOUT CLOSING THE SALE

☐ C) YOUR BELIEF IN YOUR PRODUCT OR SERVICE

☐ D) YOUR PRODUCT OR SERVICE BEING A GOOD FIT FOR THE PROSPECT

SEE ANSWER BELOW.

BEHAVIORS

IDENTIFY TWO PAST SITUATIONS WHERE YOU MAY HAVE REVEALED YOUR EMOTIONAL INVESTMENT IN THE SALE, OR BROADCAST YOUR "NEED" TO CLOSE THE SALE. WHAT ALTERNATIVE ACTIONS WOULD HAVE PROJECTED A MORE OPTIMISTIC OR CONFIDENT ATTITUDE?

Answer: B) Your confidence about closing the sale.

SANDLER
RULE #41

THERE ARE NO BAD PROSPECTS – ONLY BAD SALESPEOPLE

Have you ever blamed a lost sale on a prospect's personality or actions?

- Don't allow yourself to get caught up in the "that-guy-wouldn't-buy-from-anyone" syndrome.
- Do take responsibility.

Many salespeople have a tendency to externalize their problems, rather than accept the responsibility for what's going on in their base of business – and in their careers. Guess what? Whatever is happening in your relationship with

> WHATEVER IS HAPPENING IN THE ACCOUNT IS YOUR RESPONSIBILITY.

a prospect or customer – whether it's success or failure – is your responsibility. Whatever is happening in your career – whether you have a good territory or a bad territory, a good manager or a bad manager – is your responsibility.

At the end of the day, you are the only professional salesperson in your own world. If something gets screwed up, you and only you could have screwed it up. Don't return to your office and say, "I guess I had a personality clash with the prospect." Your job is to give the prospect any personality he needs!

Accept responsibility for your own choices and actions. This is a core principle, not only of the Sandler Selling System, but of a healthy approach to life. In the specific case of selling, it's particularly important to come to terms with this Rule, because the majority of salespeople are inclined to *avoid* assuming personal and professional responsibility when things go wrong. In most cases, salespeople externalize their problems and failures. They point the finger of blame at, among other things, the prospect, the customer, the economy, the competition, their own management, and so on. That's what *most* people are doing – including your competition. That means that you can establish a competitive and personal advantage just by building your day, and your career, around this rule. (See also Rule #35: *If Your Competition Does It, Stop Doing It Right Away.*)

It all goes back to learning from your mistakes. If you point the finger of blame at the prospect, you deprive yourself of the opportunity to learn from the mistake, which means you're destined to repeat it. Even if you keep the "blame game" to yourself – by thinking things like, "He was never going to buy," "He was a jerk," or "She was locked in," – you should know that these internal statements are depriving you of the opportunity to learn.

WHAT CAN YOU LEARN?

So: What can you learn from the "no" you just received? It shouldn't be that it was impossible to close a sale with the person you were trying to sell to. That kind of "lesson" only sets you up for failure. What else could you have done differently? What will you do differently next time? What responsibilities will you accept for what happened, or didn't happen?

Use turndowns – and other apparent obstacles – as an opportunity to sharpen your selling skills.

TEST YOUR UNDERSTANDING

WHAT DOES IT MEAN WHEN YOU FIND THAT YOU ARE DEALING WITH A PROSPECT WHO REPEATEDLY LIES, PROVIDES MISLEADING INFORMATION, REFUSES TO MAKE COMMITMENTS, AND CONTINUALLY STALLS THE PROCESS?

SEE ANSWER BELOW.

BEHAVIORS

IDENTIFY THREE SELLING SITUATIONS WHEN YOU FAILED TO TAKE RESPONSIBILITY FOR AN UNDESIRABLE OUTCOME, BUT INSTEAD BLAMED IT ON SOMEONE ELSE OR SOME EXTERNAL SITUATION. IF YOU WERE TO ACCEPT RESPONSIBILITY FOR THOSE INSTANCES RIGHT NOW, WHAT LESSONS WOULD YOU LEARN?

Answer: You are responsible for this situation. The fact that you are still dealing with a prospect who "repeatedly" engages in this behavior validates the rule.

SANDLER
RULE #42

A WINNER HAS ALTERNATIVES, A LOSER PUTS ALL HIS EGGS IN ONE BASKET

Have you ever tried to "script" a conversation with a prospect ahead of time?

- Don't try to plan the sales call word for word.

- Do keep your options open.

> THE PROSPECT HAS HIS OWN SCRIPT TO FOLLOW.

Some salespeople diligently "plan" their sales calls, sentence by sentence or even word for word. They tell themselves things like:

I'll start by saying …
Then, I'll present …
Next, I'll ask …
The prospect will likely say …
Then, I'll bring up …
The prospect's reaction will probably be …
Then, I'll respond by saying …

And so on.

Planning your sales calls, step by step, can be beneficial … as long as you don't try to stick to the script, word for word, when it's actually time to interact with the prospect.

Bear in mind that, while you have your script, your prospect also has one of his own. The chances that the two scripts will mesh smoothly – or, at any rate, in a way that gets you closer to the bank – are extremely small. Trying to stick to your "script" word for word puts unnecessary pressure on your prospect and yourself, and hinders the flow of information in both directions. Fixating on the language of your script needlessly limits your options. You have one path to walk down, and only one. That kind of selling puts all your eggs in one basket. It's not how winners operate!

KEEP YOUR OPTIONS OPEN

Sales calls are all about keeping your options open, not about nailing down a specific sequence of events – or words. If all your pre-call planning helps you to keep an open mind, open doors and respond spontaneously to opportunities, then some scripting may be a good idea as a form of preparation. Often, however, we use scripting for a very different purpose, namely, to convince ourselves that we know exactly what specific exchanges will come up when we call a given prospect. This kind of "preparation" almost always does more harm than good. We'd probably be better off sending our prospect a copy of the script ahead of time, indicating the reactions and responses we'd like to hear!

A better strategy would be to map out your call by identifying the key points you need to cover and the critical information you need to obtain. It may be helpful for you to devise some key questions to lead into each point. Rehearse your questions, but don't lock yourself into a sequence or restrict yourself only to the planned topics. Be flexible. If your prospect brings up a topic or previously undisclosed concern that is relevant to a product or service you can provide, pursue it. Allowing yourself to deviate from your initial plan and follow a new path may just be what it takes to get you to the bank!

TEST YOUR UNDERSTANDING

WHAT ARE THE MAJOR DRAWBACKS TO PLANNING YOUR SALES CALLS AROUND A PRE-PLANNED SCRIPT?

SEE ANSWER BELOW.

BEHAVIORS

TO AVOID BECOMING LOCKED INTO A SCRIPTED APPROACH, MAP OUT — IN WHATEVER FASHION THAT'S MOST COMFORTABLE TO YOU — THE PRIMARY ELEMENTS OF AN INITIAL CALL WITH A PROSPECT. NEXT, DEVELOP BULLET POINTS TO ADDRESS EACH PRIMARY ELEMENT. FINALLY, DEVELOP THE KEY QUESTIONS TO LEAD YOU INTO EACH ELEMENT, WHATEVER ORDER YOU END UP FOLLOWING.

BY INTERNALIZING THE "MAP," RATHER THAN MEMORIZING A STEP-BY-STEP SCRIPT, YOU MAINTAIN ENOUGH FLEXIBILITY TO MOVE BETWEEN TOPICS AND GATHER NEW INFORMATION AS NECESSARY.

Answer: Such a strategy locks you into a pre-planned dialogue that is not likely to be consistent with the prospect's "script." This limits the flow of information and increases the likelihood of missing out on the opportunities that only surface in a more flexible environment.

SANDLER
RULE #43

YOU DON'T LEARN HOW TO WIN BY GETTING A "YES" – YOU LEARN HOW TO WIN BY GETTING A "NO"

Do you ever fear the word "No" from prospects and customers?

- Change your focus!
- Don't fear the NO.

Getting a YES from a prospect, as in "YES, I will buy from you," takes you to the bank. That's something every salesperson will agree is a positive.

Getting a YES from a prospect also feels great. No one will argue with that, either.

Getting a YES gives you more confidence and self-assurance. That's certainly a good thing, too!

Unfortunately, most salespeople get a NO answer much more often than they get a YES answer. That's a fact of sales life. Here's another fact: If the inevitability of NO answers demotivates you, makes you feel small, keeps you from learning and improving, you need to change your focus. You need to start looking at the NO answer a little differently.

ONE SIMPLE CHANGE

We have seen many, many salespeople who were not doing at all well turn on a dime and begin generating the revenue they targeted for themselves … just by making one simple change in the way that they looked at what they did for a living. The change was this: They went into the field looking for a NO answer, rather than a YES answer. And that single, momentous change transformed their careers.

Understand: They made this change knowing they had a professional responsibility not to take any form of "Let me think it over" as an answer from a prospect! Their goal was simply to pile up a big collection of clear NO answers … on their way to the eventual YES answers. That's what allowed them to turn things around.

Show me a salesperson with ten NO answers in a row, and I'll show you someone who's close to a YES. When you set yourself up for a "win" by getting a NO, you can actually feel good about a negative result.

At one of our sales training sessions, one salesperson who was on the brink of leaving the profession grabbed hold of this idea. He decided to go after the NO – not the "maybe," mind you, but the NO – instead of the YES. He reported back to the group that he found most prospects "could not" say NO! With some gentle "pressure," he had made three sales in the week after he left the meeting!

A fringe benefit emerged. His fear of cold calling had completely disappeared! The pressure of getting a YES had been eliminated.

How can you move yourself into the winner's circle? By taking the pressure off yourself! Stop making it your job to generate some mythical rejection-free stream of YES answers – and consider it your mission to accumulate as many clear NO answers as you possibly can!

David Mattson

TEST YOUR UNDERSTANDING

CAN YOU GIVE THREE REASONS FOR NOT FEARING "NO?"

SEE ANSWER BELOW.

BEHAVIORS

IF, IN YOUR ATTEMPT TO AVOID GETTING A "NO," YOU'VE BEEN ACCEPTING "MAYBE'S," "THINK-IT-OVER'S," OR ANY OTHER WISHY-WASHY RESPONSES FROM PROSPECTS, MAKE A FIRM COMMITMENT TO STOP. WHEN YOU ASK A PROSPECT TO MAKE A DECISION, WHETHER IT'S TO GRANT YOU AN APPOINTMENT OR MAKE A BUYING DECISION, GET A "YES" OR GET A "NO." ACCEPTING A "NO" FREES YOU UP TO PURSUE MORE VIABLE OPPORTUNITIES.

Answer: 1. "No" is inevitable – not everyone you talk to will grant you an appointment or buy your product so you might as well get used to it. 2. You will hear more "no" answers than "yes" answers – there's no sense in hiding from them. 3. "No" is better than a "think-it-over" or a "maybe."

173

SANDLER
RULE #44

WHEN YOUR FOOT HURTS, YOU'RE PROBABLY STANDING ON YOUR OWN TOE

Have you ever blamed someone or something for a mistake that <u>you</u> made?

- Take responsibility when something goes wrong.
- Don't even think about blaming the prospect.

> ARE YOU
> YOUR OWN
> WORST ENEMY?

Facing a problem in the sales process? Be honest with yourself. Whose problem is it, really?

Salespeople can sometimes be their own worst enemy, creating roadblocks and detours that prevent their own efforts from moving forward. All too often, they are tempted to blame the prospect for these occurrences. This is a little like standing on your own toe, and looking around for the person who's making your foot hurt. Whenever you encounter an unpleasant surprise in your sales, you must ask yourself: whose responsibility was it to uncover this problem in the first place?

You shouldn't become angry with a prospect for doing something that appears to stall the process … when it is your responsibility to discuss the potential roadblock in advance. Don't even think about blaming the prospect! This is your problem.

AN UNPLEASANT SURPRISE

Here's an example. At the conclusion of your presentation, your prospect reveals that she is extremely impressed with your presentation. You believe you're about to close the sale. Then she informs you that she will give you a decision in a few days – just as soon as she reviews your information with the procurement committee.

Your stomach suddenly does a somersault, and your jaw clenches. You think: "Committee! What committee? You didn't tell me about any committee! Why on earth am I only learning about this now?"

That's a good question. The answer is simple: You're only learning about this now because you didn't find out enough about how the organization bought in the past. You didn't ask the right questions!

As a result, you can't get angry with the prospect for not telling you about the committee ... but you can take personal responsibility for not finding out how the buying decision would be made, and who else in addition to the prospect would have to be involved in making that decision.

It really is your job to identify and discuss potential roadblocks with your prospect before you run into those roadblocks. Past experiences are good indicators of future roadblocks you may encounter. If you run into an unpleasant surprise along the way ... that can only mean that you didn't do your job before trying to move forward!

Take responsibility. Resolve to ask better questions. Figure out what happened the last time they bought something like this. Once you know what the possible roadblocks are, you can decide on a course of action that serves both parties. You'll have more control over your selling efforts, the economic results will be more favorable ... and your foot won't hurt so much. (See also Rule #41: *There Are No Bad Prospects, Only Bad Salespeople.*)

```
┌─────────────────────────────────────────┐
│                                           │
│          TEST YOUR                        │
│       UNDERSTANDING                       │
│                                           │
│                                           │
│           HOW DO YOU                      │
│       AVOID "STANDING                     │
│     ON YOUR OWN TOE?"                     │
│                                           │
└─────────────────────────────────────────┘
```

SEE ANSWER BELOW.

BEHAVIORS

IDENTIFY THREE SITUATIONS WHERE THE PROSPECT "SURPRISED" YOU WITH SOME UNFAVORABLE OR UNEXPECTED INFORMATION THAT KEPT YOU FROM MOVING FORWARD. DETERMINE WHAT YOU COULD HAVE DONE PRIOR TO THOSE SITUATIONS TO HAVE AT LEAST UNCOVERED, OR BETTER YET, PREVENTED, THE SITUATIONS FROM OCCURRING.

Answer: Make sure that you cover, in detail, every facet of the sale. It is your responsibility to uncover potential deal-breakers before they occur, not the prospect's.

SANDLER
RULE #45

EXPRESS YOUR FEELINGS THROUGH THIRD-PARTY STORIES

Have you ever been in front of a prospect and found yourself in a situation where you felt something, but were afraid to say it out loud?

- Trust your "gut."

- Can you say what you really feel – and also move the sale forward?

How many times have you had a gut feeling about a situation but you were hesitant to say something to the prospect? Maybe there's a way to express that feeling – and support your own sales process at the same time.

For example, say your prospect is putting a lot of pressure on you because of your product's or service's price. Rather than "defending" your position – which won't work anyway – what would happen if you found a way to tell your prospect how you felt, based on something similar that has happened in your world?

For instance: "George, I appreciate your problem and I believe that I can help you solve it. I must admit, however, that I'm feeling a bit uncomfortable. You see, last week I was working with a prospective client who had committed to our program if I could obtain a favorable rate for one element of the coverage. I bent over backward to get the home office to obtain the rate for him. Then, he used our rate as leverage to get his existing broker to lower their rate. And, of course, he kept his business with them. If I can get the home office to get the rate approval needed to solve your problem, am I going to end up regretting it?"

The very best salespeople know that their work is rooted in relationships, and that relationships inevitably connect to feelings. When you have the instinct to talk about how you feel with a prospect or customer, don't let fear keep you from finding an appropriate way to do that. Usually, sharing your feelings in a professional way will strengthen the relationship — and clarify the commitments that make that relationship work for both parties.

```
┌─────────────────────────────────────┐
│                                       │
│         TEST YOUR                     │
│      UNDERSTANDING                    │
│                                       │
│                                       │
│          WHY ARE                      │
│        THIRD-PARTY                    │
│         STORIES AN                    │
│     EFFECTIVE STRATEGY                │
│       FOR EXPRESSING                  │
│        YOUR FEELINGS?                 │
│                                       │
└─────────────────────────────────────┘
```

SEE ANSWER BELOW.

BEHAVIORS

IDENTIFY TWO SELLING SITUATIONS WHERE YOU COULD HAVE USED THIRD-PARTY STORIES TO EXPRESS YOUR FEELINGS OR CONCERNS. WRITE DOWN WHAT YOU COULD HAVE SAID IN EACH CASE.

Answer: The third-party story allows the prospect to judge the salesperson's feelings from an objective point of view, since the story involves someone else.

SANDLER
RULE #46

THERE IS NO SUCH THING AS A GOOD TRY

Have you ever found yourself using "weasel words" with a prospect or customer?

- Do or don't.
- Experiment.

Let's conduct an experiment. In a moment, I want you to stop reading and try to close this book. After you've closed the book, count to 10 and reopen the book; then continue from where you left off. Remember to note the page number.

On your mark, get set ... go! Try to close the book. Go ahead ... give it a good try.

Did you close the book?

If you did, you didn't try, you actually did close the book.

If you didn't close the book, it's because you didn't try.

Confused? Don't be. Just remember Yoda's words from *The Empire Strikes Back:*

"Do. Or do not. There is no try."

Here's the point. Yoda was right. There is no "try." You either do something or you don't. "Try" is a weaselly word. At best, "try" communicates an intention, not a commitment.

> THERE IS
> NO "TRY."

With this point in mind, consider the following statements:

- "I'll try to make some prospecting calls today."
- "I'll try to get back to the prospect this week."
- "I'll try to get a decision from the prospect before the end of the month."
- "I'll try to get that report done by tomorrow afternoon."

You either schedule time for the activity, then do it … or you don't. There is no in-between. Suppose we extended the "try" concept to other areas of our lives:

- "I'll try to stop for the red traffic light."
- "I'll try to love my children."
- "I'll try to look both ways before crossing the street."

When the outcome is important, we leave "try" out of the equation.

DON'T TRY – COMMIT

The next time you're about to say that you'll "try" something, reconsider your approach. If the outcome of the activity is important, don't try; instead, commit. If the activity isn't important, then why even try?

TEST YOUR UNDERSTANDING

WHY IS "TRY" A WEASELLY WORD?

SEE ANSWER BELOW.

BEHAVIORS

BECOME MORE AWARE OF THE WAYS YOU AND YOUR PROSPECTS USE THE WORD "TRY." RATHER THAN "TRY," MAKE A CLEAR COMMITMENT. WHEN YOUR PROSPECTS OR CUSTOMERS USE THE WORD, ASK THEM WHAT THEY MEAN AND GENTLY PRESS THEM FOR A COMMITMENT.

Answer: "Try" is a weaselly word because when you only commit to "try" to do something, you're making no commitment at all.

SANDLER
RULE #47

SELLING IS A BROADWAY PLAY PERFORMED BY A PSYCHIATRIST

Have you ever lost your objectivity with a prospect or customer?

- Don't get emotionally involved.

- Do maintain your objectivity.

- Do understand, and plan for, the human dynamics you will encounter.

Buying is inevitably an emotional experience for the prospect. And selling is, all too often, an even *more* emotional experience for the salesperson.

Why can emotion be such a problem for the salesperson? Because getting emotionally involved in a selling situation can cloud your thinking. Here's how it starts: You begin to believe you are moving toward the close. Then you feel exhilarated. Then you get careless. Then you miss something. And somehow the sale slips away. Unfortunately, this is not at all an unusual chain of events!

To get an idea of the importance of keeping your composure and maintaining your objectivity, consider the relationship between a psychiatrist and his patient. During a session, the patient suddenly leaps to his feet, grabs a letter opener from the psychiatrist desk, and screams, *"I'm going to kill you!"*

Faced with this situation, the good psychiatrist does not cry out, in response, "Why me?"

Instead, he maintains an objective view of the situation, and asks himself, "Now, why is this person acting this way?" He then responds, "Tom, you're obviously upset. Before you lunge at me and do something you're sure to regret, can we talk about what's upsetting you? Perhaps there's a better way to deal with whatever you're feeling. Are you open to finding out?"

The "Why me?" response is in fact the most likely to get the psychiatrist killed. The objective response is the most likely to save his life.

You, too, must keep maintaining an objective view of the selling situation. Save your emotional enthusiasm for after the sale. During the selling process, take a "third-party" position. Look at what is going on as though you were an observer at the selling event. The buyer (your prospect) and the seller (you) are the players. *You are the director!*

> YOU MUST HAVE AN UNDERSTANDING OF HUMAN DYNAMICS.

GUIDE YOUR OWN BEHAVIOR

To be an effective professional seller, you must have an understanding of human dynamics, and you must learn to use that understanding to guide your own behavior and actions toward the best possible outcome for yourself and your prospect. That may require you to act differently with a prospect than you normally would. Again: *Give the prospect any personality he or she wants!* (See also Rule #41, *There Are No Bad Prospects, Only Bad Salespeople.*)

If you are working with a "big picture" person – you will have to focus on the grand vision, just as your prospect does, and you will have to make sure that high-level issues are given prominence over procedural details that you know this person will be bored with (and end up handing off to others). On the other hand, if you are working with a perpetual "fact-checker," you will want to "play the part" of the salesperson who knows how to dot every "i" and cross every "t."

Your interaction with the prospect – from the moment you say "hello" to the moment the contract is signed, and in all the moments that follow – will inevitably be governed by certain "rules of engagement." It is your job to discover the rules, which will be unique to each relationship. Think of the job of identifying and following those rules the way you would think of the job of giving a great performance in a Broadway play – a performance where you, the leading actor, happen to have all the knowledge, credentials, and experience, of a great psychiatrist. That background could come in handy if your costar should ever start behaving erratically.

TEST YOUR UNDERSTANDING

WHY IS IT BENEFICIAL TO MAINTAIN THE DIRECTOR'S OBJECTIVE VIEW OF YOUR SELLING INTERACTIONS?

SEE ANSWER BELOW.

BEHAVIORS

IDENTIFY TWO SITUATIONS WHERE YOU BECAME EMOTIONALLY INVOLVED IN THE SELLING PROCESS — SITUATIONS WHERE YOU WERE RELUCTANT TO ACCEPT THE PROSPECT'S POINT OF VIEW, FOR INSTANCE — AND YOUR OWN RESPONSES DID NOT HELP YOU MOVE THE SALE FORWARD.

WHAT COULD YOU HAVE DONE DIFFERENTLY, AND MORE OBJECTIVELY, IN EACH SITUATION?

Answer: By maintaining an objective viewpoint, you are less likely to become emotionally connected to the process. Assuming an emotional position can color your judgment and prevent you from responding effectively and taking appropriate actions.

SANDLER
RULE #48

A LIFE WITHOUT RISK IS A LIFE WITHOUT GROWTH

Have you ever felt as though you were being left behind ... because you were unwilling to learn and attempt new things?

- Keep reaching.
- Don't get complacent.
- Don't stop learning.

Hallelujah! Things are going well – or, at least, well enough. You can finally exhale! Repeat orders from your existing customers are getting you close enough to your monthly quota to keep your sales manager off your back. You are relatively happy with the predictable amount of your monthly commission checks. Why risk changing what's working for you? After all, life is good now ... right?

Actually, you might not want to "get too comfortable" quite yet. Your best customers are, right now, at the top of your competitors' prospect lists. New products, services, and technologies are hitting the market that are about to transform your world. Decision makers with whom you've built up great relationships are getting

> YOU ARE EITHER GROWING AS A SALESPERSON OR YOU ARE DYING.

ready to change positions, move on to new companies, or retire. Things in your territory could change overnight, and, if the past is any indication, they probably will. If you kick back now, and take the next quarter off for that long professional nap you've been promising yourself, you will find that the inevitable task of making sense of the world you wake up to will be very difficult indeed.

You can't afford to cling to the status quo. It's an illusion, anyway. Everything's actually changing, and that means you might as well change, too, if you plan to keep up. If change is inevitable, and it is, why not find a way to change for the better? To paraphrase Bob Dylan: You are either growing as a salesperson, or you are dying. There is no in between. Don't get left behind!

If you want to keep growing, you'll need to take some risks. What, exactly, will you have to risk? First and foremost, you will have to risk the habit of "coasting" on your past achievements. That's called complacency, and it's a bad destination for a salesperson – or any other kind of person. Living in complacency full-time is, paradoxically enough, the biggest risk of all.

None of the other "risks" you are likely to experience as a salesperson – the gatekeeper who pushes you away, the prospect who tunes out of a great presentation – are as threatening in the long term as complacency, though some may bruise your ego. However, if you resolve to *learn* from as many of your experiences as possible, you will become stronger with every experience, and your life will become *richer*.

If you're not willing to take a risk, you're not going to move forward from where you are. So be willing to take the risk of reaching for something you're not yet sure of, something that you think might just be better than what you've got now. Even if you don't get exactly the results you're after, you will learn a lesson that will help you next time around – and you will grow.

TEST YOUR UNDERSTANDING

WHY MUST YOU "RISK" IF YOU INTEND TO GROW?

SEE ANSWER BELOW.

BEHAVIORS

IDENTIFY TWO AREAS WHERE YOU FEEL YOU MAY HAVE BEEN COASTING IN THE PAST, PROFESSIONALLY SPEAKING. THEN, FOR EACH INSTANCE, IDENTIFY ONE THING YOU CAN DO TO STRETCH YOURSELF AND GROW ... AND THEN SET A DATE TO BEGIN.

Answer: The sales arena is a dynamic and competitive place. If you're not willing to stretch and try new things, you'll get left behind!

SANDLER
RULE #49

LEAVE YOUR CHILD
IN THE CAR

*Have you ever let your emotions get the
better of you in a selling situation?*

- Let's revisit Transactional Analysis.

- Nurture your prospect's Child.

- Supress the salesperson's Child.

At the beginning of this book, you were introduced to Transactional
Analysis (T-A), the human relations model that David Sandler used
as a foundation for developing the Sandler Selling System training
methodology. You discovered how each of the three ego states – Parent,
Adult, and Child – influenced the prospect's behavior and, ultimately,
the buying decision. Now, let's see how each of those ego states can
influence the *salesperson*.

As you'll recall, the Parent ego state is where we store right/wrong, do/
don't, should/shouldn't, and similar lessons and messages we received
from our parents and other authority figures as we were growing up
– lessons and messages that now largely control our judgments and
behavior. Sometimes, those messages were delivered in a "critical" way –
in a stern and authoritarian manner. At other times, they were delivered
in a more "nurturing" manner – as helpful suggestions and words of
encouragement.

You'll remember, too, that the Adult ego state is the "computer" part of our makeup: data in, data out. This ego state facilitates objective, logical, and unemotional analysis and decision-making.

The Child ego state, you'll recall, is where we stored our feelings about the rights and wrongs, the shoulds and shouldn'ts, and the dos and don'ts that Mom and Dad were teaching, preaching, and demanding. At times, the Child could be very accommodating when it came to receiving these messages – sometimes, merely in an attempt to gain approval and acceptance. At other times, the Child could be downright rebellious, resisting the messages or defying them outright. Every parent has experienced, at least once, the spectacle of a young child dropping to the floor, kicking his feet and screaming when he couldn't get his way.

As you learned in the opening pages of this book, David Sandler recognized that salespeople had to engage all three aspects of the prospect's makeup – the Parent, the Adult, and the Child – when developing a selling opportunity. The Child must want what you have to sell. The Adult must conclude that logically, it is appropriate to obtain it. And the Parent must give the Child permission to have it.

> YOUR CHILD MUST PLAY NO PART IN THE SELLING PROCESS.

Sandler also made some conclusions about ego states that were of interest to professional salespeople. While the prospect's Child is the critical element on the prospect's side of the buyer-seller interaction, Sandler taught that the *salesperson's* Child must play *no* part in the process. The salesperson should neither be looking for approval nor acceptance from his prospect (See Rule # 20, *The Bottom Line of Professional Selling is Going to the Bank*) nor should he begin "kicking and screaming" when things aren't going his way. Otherwise, it will be impossible for the salesperson to remain objective and keep emotions in check.

Sandler concluded that most of your interaction with prospects – about 70 percent – should come from your "nurturing" Parent and the remaining 30 percent should come from your Adult. During a sales call, the salesperson's Child must remain in the car! (You can reacquaint yourself with this ego state after the meeting, perhaps by pumping your fist in the air and shouting something like "Fantastic!" after having closed the sale.)

TEST YOUR UNDERSTANDING

WHY IS THE SALES ARENA NO PLACE FOR YOUR "CHILD?"

SEE ANSWER BELOW.

BEHAVIORS

IDENTIFY THREE COMMON SITUATIONS DURING THE SELLING PROCESS WHERE YOUR ACTIONS AND REACTIONS MAY BE GUIDED MORE BY YOUR EMOTION THAN YOUR INTELLECT. FOR EACH INSTANCE, IDENTIFY A DIFFERENT COURSE OF ACTION – ONE GUIDED BY A LOGICAL, RATHER THAN EMOTIONAL, ASSESSMENT OF THE SITUATION.

Answer: To function effectively and analyze selling situations and solutions, the salesperson must maintain an objective point of view. In order to do that, he must keep his emotions in check.

EPILOGUE

SOME FINAL THOUGHTS ON GOOD TIMES, BAD TIMES, AND THE BEHAVIORS BEHIND THEM

In the opening lines of *A Tale of Two Cities*, Charles Dickens wrote: "It was the best of times, it was the worst of times; ... we had everything before us, we had nothing before us ..."

Somehow, that passage evokes the inescapable ups and downs of the sales profession. There will be periods when you feel you are in the "best of times," periods when you have everything before you – unlimited opportunities, responsive prospects, repeat customers, and numerous referrals. Life couldn't be any better.

Then there will be periods that feel like the "worst of times" – times when it feels like you have nothing before you. Prospects won't take your calls. Customers cut back on orders. The supply of leads from the marketing department dries up. In Dickens' words, your "spring of hope" turns to your "winter of despair."

During your "worst of times," you can give up, sit on the sidelines, and wait for things to get better. Or you can knuckle down and do what needs to be done to search out and identify, qualify, and develop new, viable opportunities. Is it harder to develop business opportunities when prospects aren't lining up at the door? Certainly. Is it impossible? No. It just takes dedication – and enough discipline to do the necessary behaviors.

If you pick up the phone and start dialing, you will, miracle of miracles, eventually find yourself in the middle of discussions. Knowing what you know, you can turn those discussions into prospecting calls.

If you make enough prospecting calls, you'll find prospects.

If you ask enough prospects to make commitments and buying decisions, you'll obtain commitments and buying decisions.

If your behaviors are correct and consistent, the results will follow.

THE DICKENS PARADOX

There is a puzzling issue to consider in any discussion of the "best of times" and the "worst of times." It is this: If we are not careful, our "best of times" may actually prove to be our undoing as salespeople.

After all, it is during the "best of times" that we may begin to let our most productive, proactive behaviors slip. When our prospects are plentiful and demand for our products and services is high, we may not feel compelled to maintain the same respect for our own prospecting routines that we had previously. When there are plenty of opportunities in the pipeline and many presentations scheduled, we are more likely to let a prospect slide on a commitment, more likely to accept a "think it over" – rather than be firm about obtaining a decision. When times seem good, we may allow the relationships that got us through the "worst of times" to become stale or disappear. We make the comfortable, but lethal, shift from proactive behavior patterns to reactive behavior patterns.

During the best of times, we salespeople can become sloppy – and still do quite well. Eventually, however, the tide will turn. And the behaviors that would have prevented our income from plummeting will no longer be second nature to us. We will have to work hard to make them second nature all over again ... if we plan to make our way back to the "best of times."

Performing the appropriate, proactive behaviors *consistently* is the key to maximizing your success during the best of times – and the key to maintaining a consistently high income level, even during the worst of times. You can solve the "Dickens Paradox" – if you resolve to remain proactive, to keep making conscious choices and performing the actions that will move you forward

Do the behaviors! Do the behaviors! Do the behaviors!

– David Mattson

INDEX

CONGRATULATIONS!

The Sandler Rules
includes a complimentary seminar!

Take this opportunity to personally experience the non-traditional sales training and reinforcement coaching that has been recognized internationally for decades.

Companies in the Fortune 1000 as well as thousands of small- to medium-sized businesses choose Sandler Training for sales, leadership, management, and a wealth of other skill-building programs. Now, it's your turn, and it's free!

You'll learn the latest practical, tactical, feet-in-the-street sales methods directly from your neighborhood Sandler Trainers! They're knowledgeable, friendly and informed about your local selling environment.

Here's how you redeem YOUR FREE SEMINAR invitation.

1. Go to www.sandler.com, and click on the SEARCH NOW button (upper right corner).

2. Select your location from the drop-down menus.

3. Review the list of all the Sandler trainers in your area.

4. Call your local Sandler trainer, mention The Sandler Rules, and reserve your place at the next seminar!